THE BIG BOOK OF
INVISIBLE TECHNOLOGY

THE BIG BOOK OF INVISIBLE TECHNOLOGY

A LOOK AT HOW THINGS WORK
FOR KIDS

Chloe Taylor

ROCKRIDGE PRESS

Copyright © 2020 by Rockridge Press, Emeryville, California

No part of this publication may be reproduced, stored in a retrieval system, or transmitted in any form or by any means, electronic, mechanical, photocopying, recording, scanning, or otherwise, except as permitted under Sections 107 or 108 of the 1976 United States Copyright Act, without the prior written permission of the Publisher. Requests to the Publisher for permission should be addressed to the Permissions Department, Rockridge Press, 6005 Shellmound Street, Suite 175, Emeryville, CA 94608.

Limit of Liability/Disclaimer of Warranty: The Publisher and the author make no representations or warranties with respect to the accuracy or completeness of the contents of this work and specifically disclaim all warranties, including without limitation warranties of fitness for a particular purpose. No warranty may be created or extended by sales or promotional materials. The advice and strategies contained herein may not be suitable for every situation. This work is sold with the understanding that the Publisher is not engaged in rendering medical, legal, or other professional advice or services. If professional assistance is required, the services of a competent professional person should be sought. Neither the Publisher nor the author shall be liable for damages arising herefrom. The fact that an individual, organization, or website is referred to in this work as a citation and/or potential source of further information does not mean that the author or the Publisher endorses the information the individual, organization, or website may provide or recommendations they/it may make. Further, readers should be aware that websites listed in this work may have changed or disappeared between when this work was written and when it is read.

For general information on our other products and services or to obtain technical support, please contact our Customer Care Department within the United States at (866) 744-2665, or outside the United States at (510) 253-0500.

Rockridge Press publishes its books in a variety of electronic and print formats. Some content that appears in print may not be available in electronic books, and vice versa.

TRADEMARKS: Rockridge Press and the Rockridge Press logo are trademarks or registered trademarks of Callisto Media Inc. and/or its affiliates, in the United States and other countries, and may not be used without written permission. All other trademarks are the property of their respective owners. Rockridge Press is not associated with any product or vendor mentioned in this book.

Interior and Cover Designer: Mando Daniel

Art Producer: Karen Williams

Editor: Morgan Shanahan

Production Editor: Ruth Sakata Corley

Illustration © 2020 Emily Emerson; Cover, Istock and Shutterstock; Art Collection / Alamy, p. xix; NASA Image Collection/ Alamy (3), p. xxi; Gado Images/ Alamy (Katherine Johnson), p. xxi; Kittipong Jirasukhanont/ Alamy (3-D printer), p. 33; Robert Chlopas / Almay (Laser tape measure), p. 38; manhattan_art / Alamy (ear buds) p. 41; For submit / Alamy (DPL 3d printer), p. 44; Raymond Asia Photography / Alamy, p. 47; Hugh Threlfall / Alamy, p. 67; AB Forces News Collection / Alamy, p. 99; Jiraroj Praditcharoenkul / Alamy, p. 105; Archive PL / Alamy, p. 117; Unite Images / Stocksy, p. 37; Colin Anderson / Stocksy, p. 80; All other interior photos by istock and shutterstock. Author photo courtesy of © Katelyn Perry.

ISBN: Print 978-1-64611-251-7 | eBook 978-1-64611-252-4

R0

*To my parents, Philip and Melanie Taylor.
I will love you always and forever.*

CONTENTS

Introduction viii

PART ONE Invisible Tech 1

PART TWO Tech You Can Touch 29

PART THREE Tech to the Future 81

The Future Is for You 92

Glossary 120

Resources 123

Introduction

Have you ever wondered how a robot can drive a car? Or how we can send messages from our phones to anywhere in the world instantly? Well, if you have, this book is for you. And if you haven't, it's time to get curious, and this book is sure to spark your imagination. Technology is all around us, evolving quickly and changing through time. It's easy to overlook how magical our daily lives are in the modern world. People long ago could only dream of flying across the ocean or talking face-to-face with their loved ones thousands of miles away. Today, it happens seamlessly. Do you ever think about how we got here, to this digital life, and where we will go next? Just how far can we fly? It's something I think about a lot. You could say it's kind of a passion of mine.

I love teaching people about how things work. As a kid, I was super curious about the world around me. I loved conducting science experiments in my parents' bathroom, mixing up any potions and powders that I could get my hands on. I wandered around the woods near my home, stumbling upon all kinds of wild plants, animals, and occasionally (*eek!*) insects. But the thing I loved the most was playing on my home computer. When I was in middle school, the internet started to become popular in homes and at school, and life would never be the same. Suddenly, a whole new world opened up. I could chat with friends, play games, share music, and create websites of my own. I spent all my free time on my computer; I was on it so much I'd often dream that I was online! Looking back, I probably spent too much time on the web, but sure enough, my favorite hobby became my profession. I'm still that super curious girl who loves to play with tech. But now, as an adult, my job is to help people of all ages, especially kids, learn about technology in really fun ways. I love to teach people how to communicate with machines through code and explain how robots can perform complex tasks both big and small.

In this book, you will read all about how modern tech works and, through step-by-step experiments, have an opportunity to learn firsthand how these magical methods were built, from the very basic to the super complex. Using your hands and doing your own experiments will help you make sense of how machines operate and encourage you to think through the steps they follow. Experimentation is an important part of the learning process. Ask a grown-up if they have any older devices that they'd be willing to give you for your research. You may be able to find some machines that are not being used anymore to experiment with. Challenge yourself to carefully and safely take apart an old keyboard or remote control. What do you see inside? Can you put it back together again? When you get hands-on with hardware, you may be inspired to build an invention of your own.

Because technology is always changing, the words we use to describe it change frequently, too. Important tech-related words used in this book will be highlighted in bold along with their definitions, and they will also be listed in the glossary at the back of the book so you can find them later.

Building a strong vocabulary will help you communicate your thoughts and ideas clearly to others, so make sure to keep track of the words you learn and take notes when something is new to you.

As our world becomes more advanced, it's easy to lose sight of how things work around us. A computer, a phone, or other familiar tech may seem ordinary, but we're going to explore the extraordinary ways they were built and the things they're able to do. You might see a driverless car whiz down the street or pick up your smartphone to play a game, but do you ever wonder about what makes them work? *Using* technology and *building* with technology are two different skill sets. A 21-century kid will need to understand both.

This book has three parts to help you start your journey into the world of tech. The first part, Invisible Tech, will teach you all about how computers came to communicate and connect like magic, running code and sending signals through the air. The second part, Tech You Can Touch, is focused on the tech you can see and feel: robots, 3D printers, drones, and many more devices that interact with our world. They work together with invisible tech to make machines come to life. Lastly, in Tech to the Future, we'll use what we've learned about invisible technology to bring real, visible, and important change to our lives today. We will **brainstorm**, meaning to generate ideas individually or as a group, and plan ways to positively influence our planet. Are you ready?

Modern technology has dramatically changed how we live and work. It has shaped our world in a way that we never thought possible and can be the key to solving some of Earth's biggest challenges. But that can only happen if we apply the knowledge that we have in smart ways and work together for the greater good.

So, are you ready? The future needs you.

It takes all kinds of tech to make our world run!

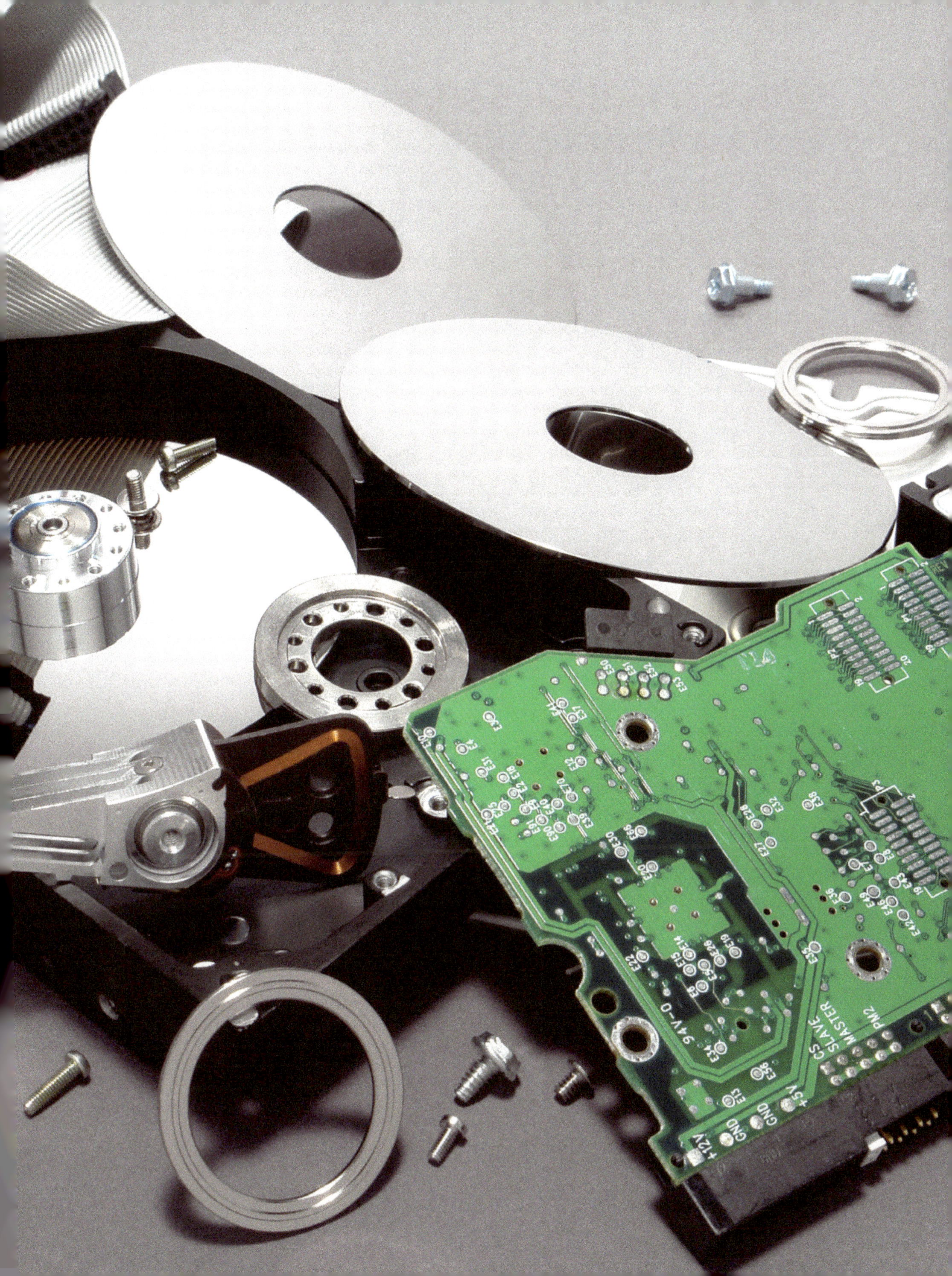
CS
SLAVE
MASTER
PM2
+12V
GND
GND
+5V

Why a New Tech Book?

This book was written to help you understand how invisible technology really works. Learning about the roots of our modern devices will give you a good sense of how we got here and where we can go in the future. Inventions like the internet, driverless cars, and Bluetooth technology seem to work on their own. However, through the experiments and investigations in this book, you will learn that there's far more to technology than what your eyes are showing you.

Screen Free Time

A big part of learning about technology is actually spent screen-free. I spend most of my time reading, writing, using physical tools and materials, brainstorming with friends, and listening to experts talk about the future. I enjoy using my computer and phone, but they're not the only way I work. The same is true about this book. In it, you'll learn a lot about how technology works, and I encourage you to talk about what you've learned with friends and to play around so that you can invent some tech of your own! Who knows? You may just stumble upon the next big **innovation**, or great new idea.

Practice the 20-20-20 rule when it comes to screen time.

One of the most important things we can do to enhance our invisible-tech-filled lives is step away from our screens from time to time. It can be hard to take breaks when screens are so easy to access, but we need time offline. The blue light that screens emit can make it hard for our brains to figure out if it is day or night, and that can disrupt our sleep patterns. Try to set a goal for some screen-free time with natural light every day. You could go for a walk or read this book outside. Maybe sit and talk with friends IRL (in real life) instead of by text. And if you do spend a lot of time in front of your devices, consider using the 20-20-20 rule to give your eyes a much-needed break. For every 20 minutes you're in front of a screen, take a break and look at something 20 feet away (about the length of two school-yard benches) for 20 seconds.

From Pictographs to Emojis

What comes to mind when you hear the word *technology*? When you think about tech today and in the future, you probably think about digital gizmos and gadgets, flying cars, and super-sophisticated robots. Yes, those are great examples of technology. But did you know that technology also includes tools we've used in the past? It's true. The past **iterations**, or versions, of our modern innovations, are important parts of tech history. An iteration can be described as a newer or better version that's created after repeating the process many times.

Humans have always had a need to communicate with each other. From our earliest interactions, we've created ways to express ourselves. Researchers believe that humans began to speak to each other around 35,000 BCE (that means language has been around a really, really long time). But what about written messages? Let's think about how early people communicated through text to learn more about how we communicate today.

Speaking to someone face-to-face and sending a quick text are completely different forms of communication. Why would you choose one method over the other? Researchers have found evidence of writing as far back as 3000 BCE, over 30,000 years after human communication first began. The oldest written language is commonly believed to be from ancient Sumer. Ancient Sumerian people lived in the heart of Mesopotamia, which is located in southern Iraq on today's maps. Many of the earliest messages were written on cave walls or into wet clay and rocks. The people of ancient Sumer needed to keep written records for their businesses, and they began by making marks to represent numbers; for example, three marks to represent three pieces of clay. Eventually, their writing became more descriptive, and the tally marks started to take on the shapes of the items they wanted them to represent. For example, Sumerians would use a drawing of a foot to represent walking or waves to communicate water. These representations were called **pictographs**, and we can think of them as ancient emojis. Over time, the pictographs got more specific, and people communicated in greater detail. Kind of like how our first emojis looked like this :) but now look like this 😎.

Ancient Egyptians kept records using images like these hieroglyphs.

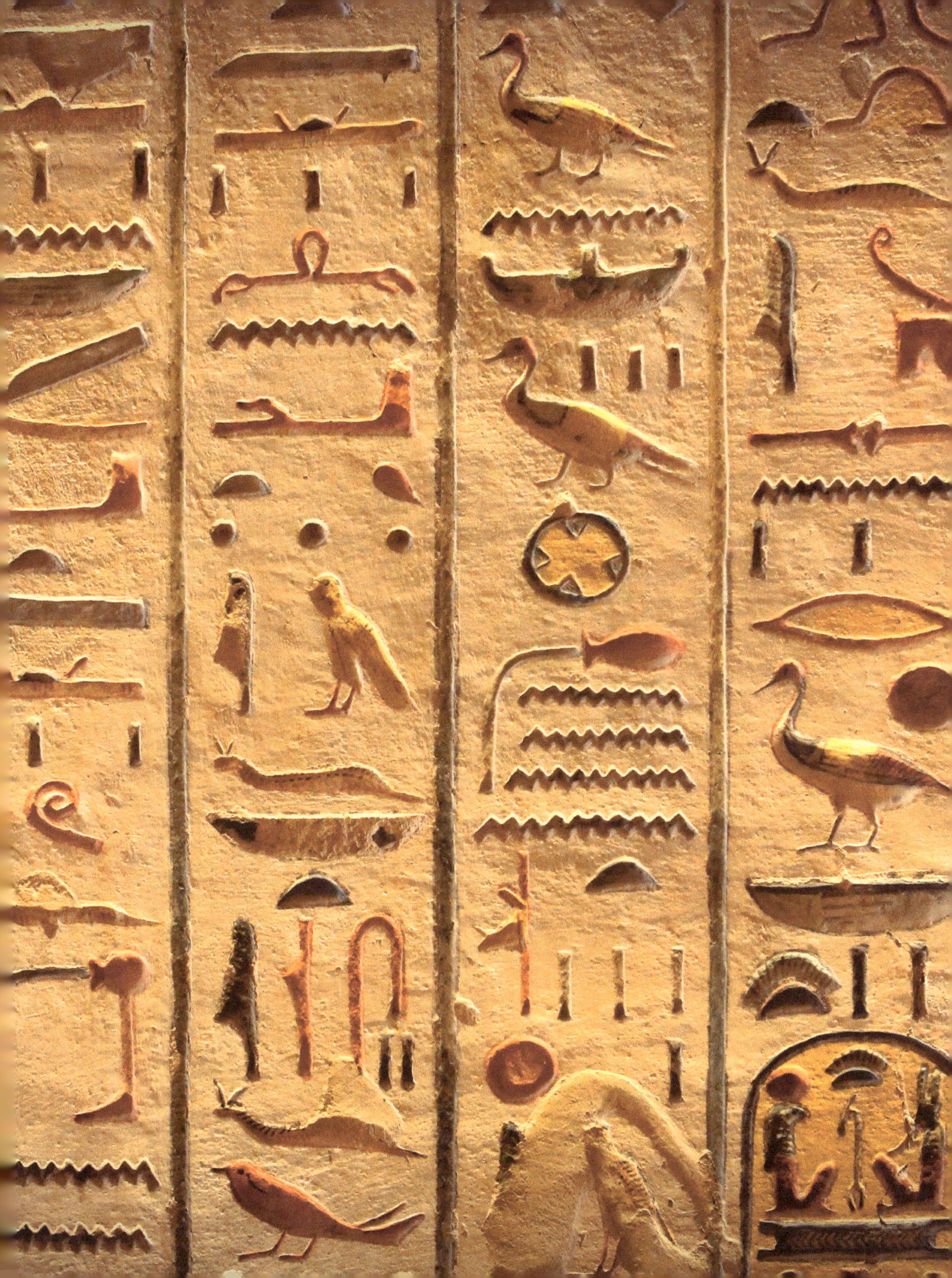

The Evolution of Code: How Did It All Begin? Where Will It Go?

To really understand any type of modern technology, we have to trace its roots all the way back to its **inception**, or creation. All of the machines we use today, and all of the inventions we will use in the future, are built based on iterations that came before. Think about the evolution of the telephone. How many iterations of the telephone have been created in the past 100 years? Early telephones were connected by long wires and needed the help of people who worked as phone operators to physically switch the lines. Early telephones worked, but there was room for improvement. Our current phones can instantly and seamlessly make calls, but could they be any better?

Now, let's think about computers. If we trace the **origin**, or history, of the computer to the beginning, it brings us to a really unlikely place: the **loom**. Yes, a loom—the thing that weaves yarn to make clothes and other fabrics. If you've ever tried to use a loom or started a knitting project, you know that the yarn you use has to be knit together in a very specific way. If you're knitting a hat, there's a pattern you have to follow to make it. And if you are weaving, especially if you're weaving a color pattern, there's a process that you follow to create that pattern. The order really matters. Long ago, all weaving was done by hand. The weaving process was time consuming and complex, but that was the way people created **textiles**, meaning clothes or other woven fabrics, across many different cultures. It's hard to imagine, but before the 1800s, if you wanted a shirt or dress or blanket, you had to weave the fabric for it from scratch.

These punch cards were used to tell the Jacquard loom what the woven pattern should look like. The loom would then read the information on the cards and follow the program to weave complex patterns.

In 1801, a Frenchman named Joseph Jacquard invented a very special loom. The Jacquard loom used paper **punch cards**—flat, rectangular pieces of paper with small holes cut out in specific patterns—as instructions for the weaving design. The placement of the holes told the loom exactly where to weave or not to weave. This meant the machine could do very complex designs just by reading the information on the cards. It is estimated that the Jacquard loom could run up to 20 times faster than previous looms, and the weaving was realistic, like a painting, which was a huge leap for weaving technology. Historians consider the Jacquard loom to be the first example of a machine acting as a computer, taking in information and giving back a desired result.

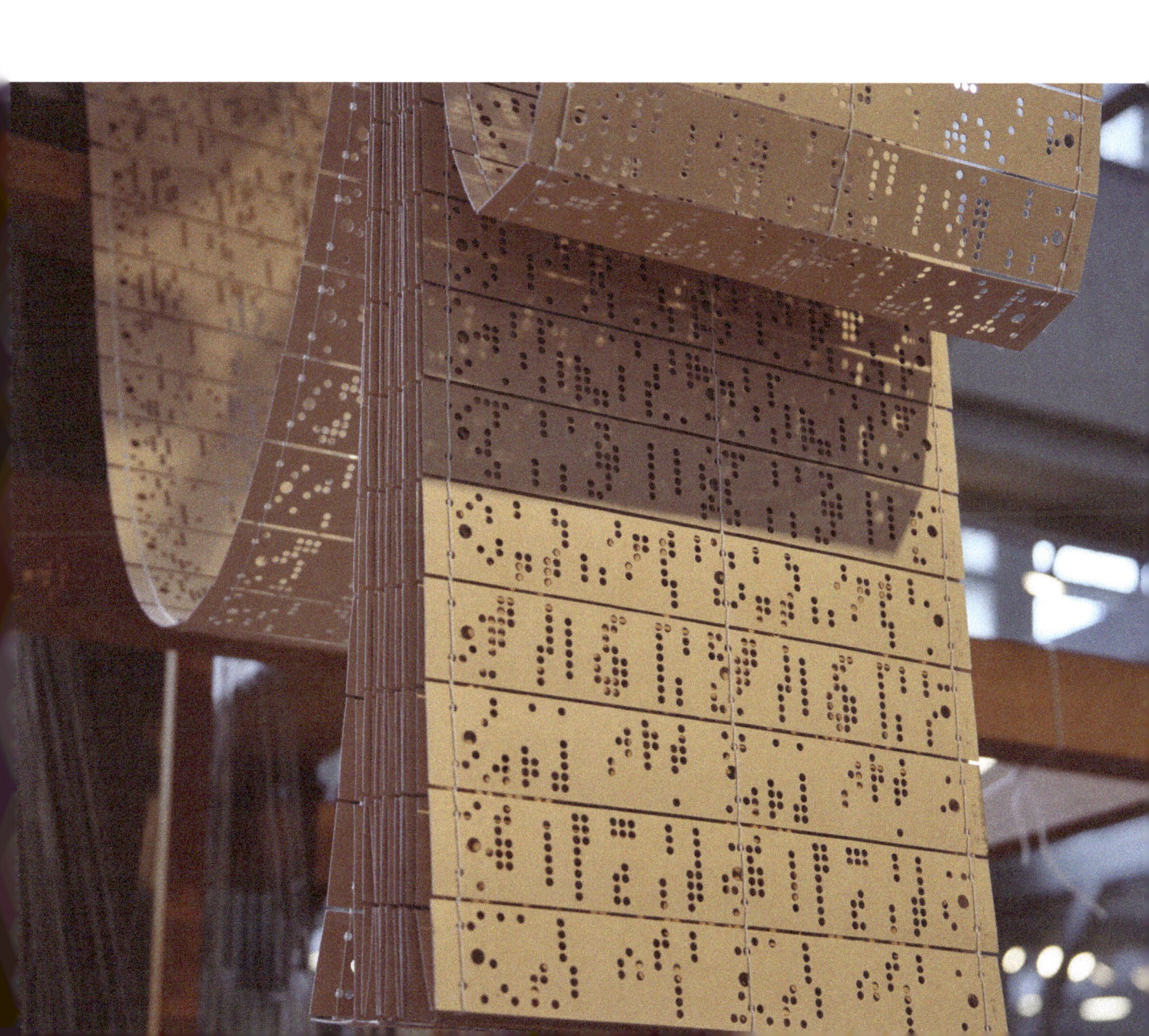

The Dawn of Computers: From Weaving to the Moon Walk

A **computer** is defined by Technopedia.com as "a machine or device that performs a process, calculation, or operation based on instructions." It allows a person to take a step back from the job at hand and let the computer do the work for them. Several years after the Jacquard loom was invented, a man named Charles Babbage took interest in how the loom worked, but he wasn't interested in weaving at all. The punch cards were the part that interested him. He wondered if punch cards could serve other purposes, like telling a machine which numbers to add or not add. The concept was revolutionary. Babbage spent years sketching out plans for how his idea could work and later enlisted the help of Ada Lovelace, who took his idea even further. She wondered if this machine would be able to weave mathematical patterns just like it was able to weave images of flowers and leaves. Lovelace is considered one of the first **computer programmers** and one of the first notable women in the creation of modern computing. You may have heard the term *computer programmer* before, because it is still used today. Simply put, a computer **program** is the set of instructions that tells a computer what to do Joseph Jacquard programmed the loom to produce a specific pattern. Ada Lovelace envisioned programs that would help us solve complex math problems in the future. Her idea wouldn't just take us into the future, it would take us to the stars. Almost 100 years after Charles Babbage and Ada Lovelace worked on their early computer in London, England, some incredible women were using their ideas to put people on the moon.

Inspired by the Jacquard loom Ada Lovelace wondered if the punch card method could be used to solve complex math problems.

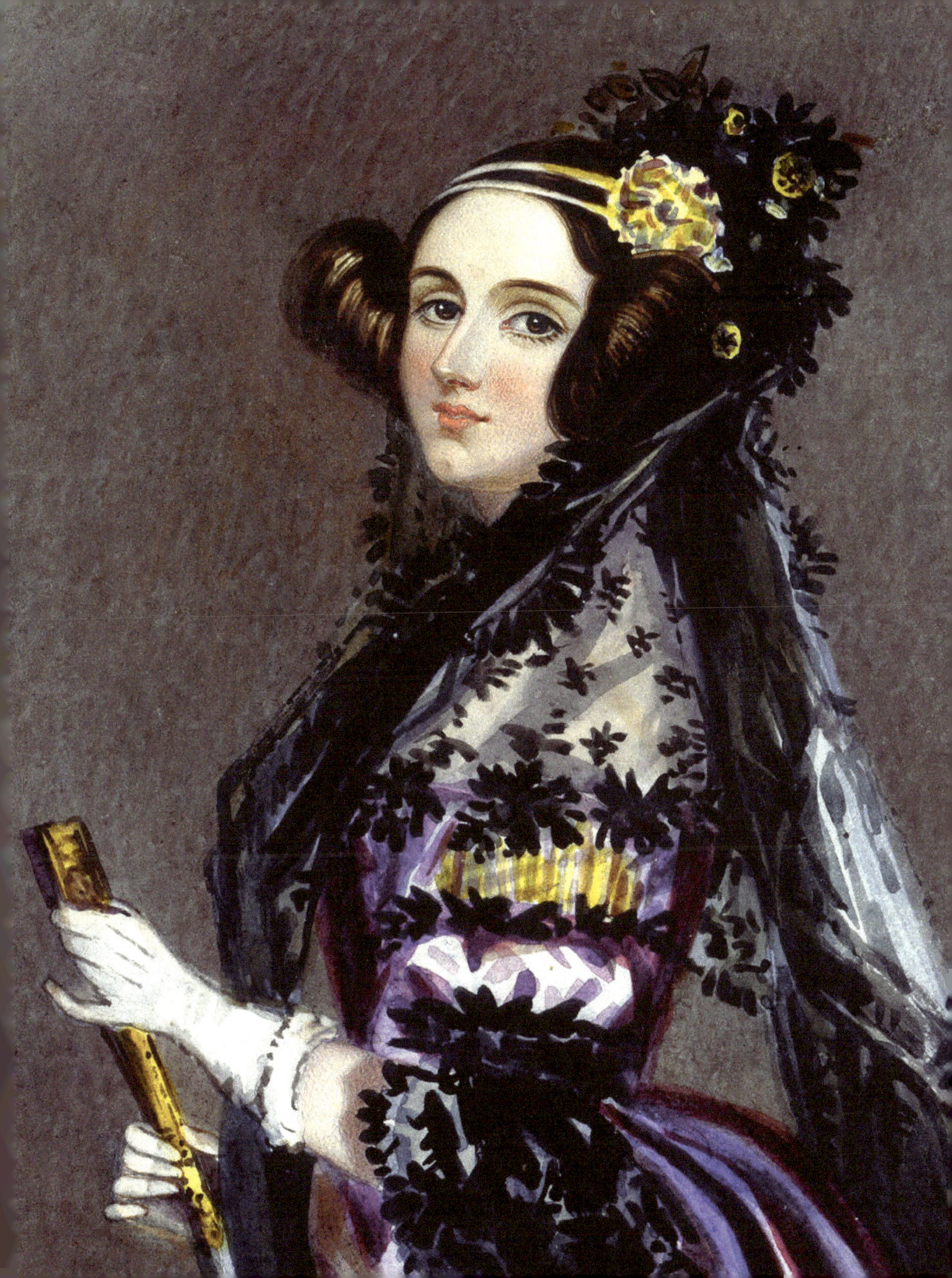

NASA's Pivotal Programmers

At NASA's Langley Laboratory during the 1950s, the space race was on, and, as you can imagine, there was a ton of math involved in making sure that space flight was successful. Originally, calculations were done by people, not machines, and a lot of people at NASA spent their days checking their calculations by hand to make sure that their answers were correct. Some of these people, like Katherine Johnson, Mary Jackson, and Dorothy Vaughan, had the extraordinary task of computing by hand and, in addition, learning how to compute with machines. The first computers, as we know them today, were created by IBM (International Business Machines), and they were far bigger than the people who worked on them. When people write programs for computers, they do so in different computer programming languages. Just like the languages you may speak with another person, programmers learn different languages to communicate with various machines. At that time, IBM computers were programmed with a language called FORmula TRANslator, or FORTRAN for short. FORTRAN helped calculate the path that astronauts would follow on their journey through space and return to Earth, but Katherine Johnson was often asked to compute the mathematical calculations by hand, just in case.

Mary Jackson worked on the calculations that took humans to the moon.

Dorothy Vaughan   Katherine Johnson   Mary Jackson

Dorothy Vaughan, Katherine Johnson, and Mary Jackson hand-checked the calculations for the route astronauts would take through space to reach the moon.

Coding 101: Get with the Program

How do we program computers today? We've come a long way from Jacquard's punch cards, but, believe it or not, some of the concepts are the same. Computers can really only understand 1s and 0s, which is called **binary code**. If we use the loom as an example, 1 could mean weave and 0 could mean don't weave. More simply, 1 = ON and 0 = OFF. These 1s and 0s are the smallest pieces of information that a computer can understand, so when we program them today, we are essentially telling them very complex directions broken down in little bits that they can comprehend. Binary code is too long and complex for us to write for our computers. Instead, we have programming languages that make the process of communicating with them much easier.

If you'd like to begin writing your first lines of code, you can use a block-based coding software like Scratch. Block-based coding is a great way to get started writing easy programs on your computer. Each block represents a step in your program, and you can experiment with what will happen when it runs. After getting the hang of block-based coding, you may want to try text-based coding. Most programming languages that are used to build websites, apps, and other digital products are built with lines of text-based code.

Binary code is a way of breaking down the complex instructions we give our computers into tiny bits of information they can understand.

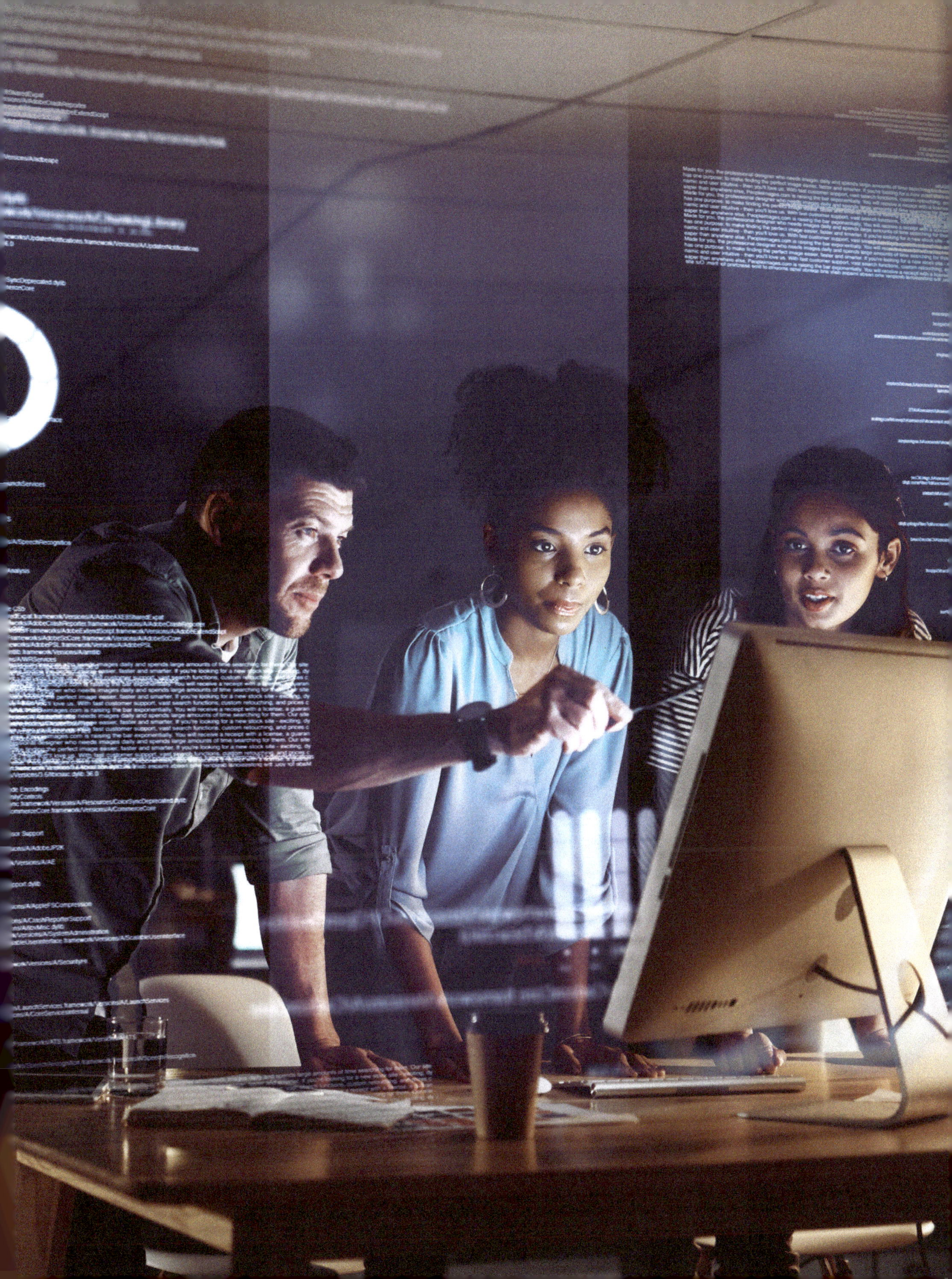

Technobabble: The Many Languages of Programming

There are so many different programming languages, and there's so much you can learn. Interested in building your own website? You'll want to check out HTML, JavaScript, and CSS. Want to build an app for an iPhone? Try Swift. If working with robots is your thing, start researching Python and C++. Learning to code is an important skill to have as we enter a truly digital age. Coding helps you think in new and creative ways. It's challenging, and once you get the hang of it, you'll be able to make your own digital projects. Give it a try!

Getting Connected

It's human nature to interact with one another, so it makes sense that building our computers to do the same became the next step in the internet story. While computers could help us with our own day-to-day needs, eventually programmers saw the potential for connecting with *other* computers, like playing a game or sending a message.

Today, programmers have learned to communicate with computers through many, many coding languages for different applications.

Hyper Text Markup Language

Cascading Style Sheets

JavaScript

5

3

JS

HTML tells your browser what a website should look like including fonts, colors, links, and location of the images that appear on the site.

CSS works alongside HTML and other coding languages to adapt the design of a website to fit on your mobile device or adjust to the size of your computer screen.

JavaScript can take a HTML website to the next level by allowing coders to create elements and cool visual effects that respond when the user interacts with them.

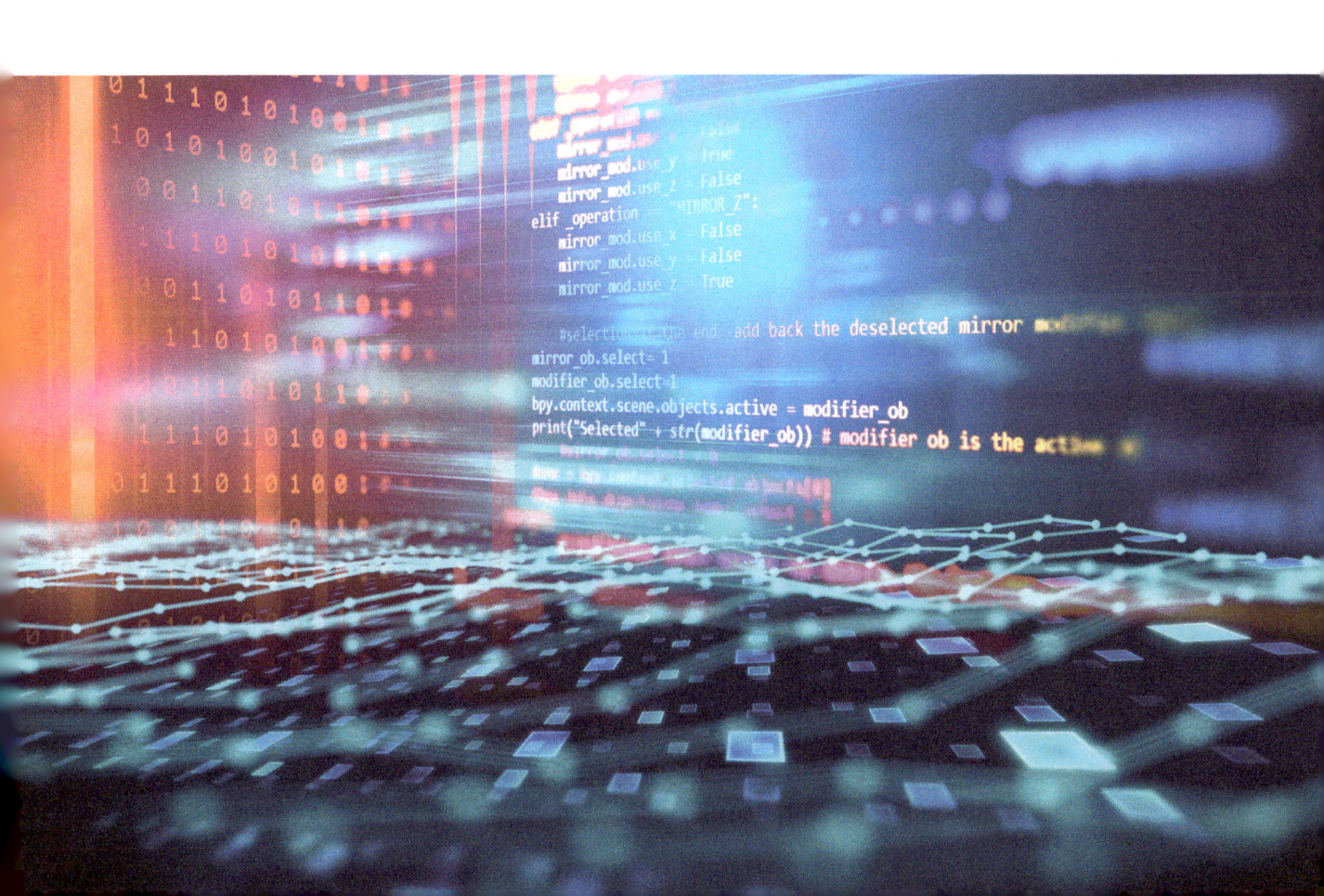

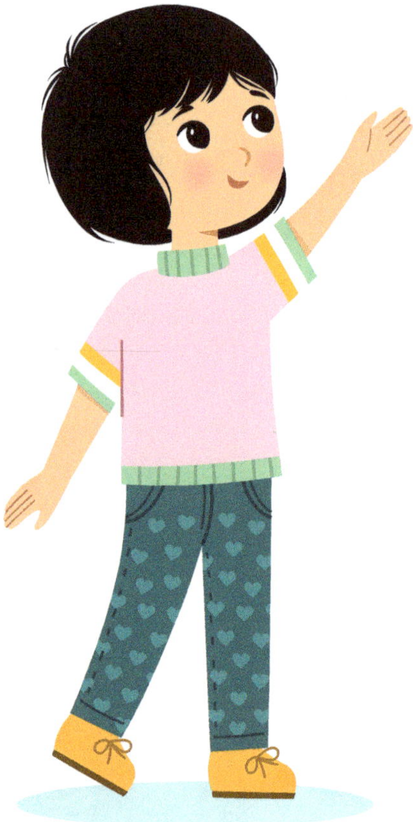

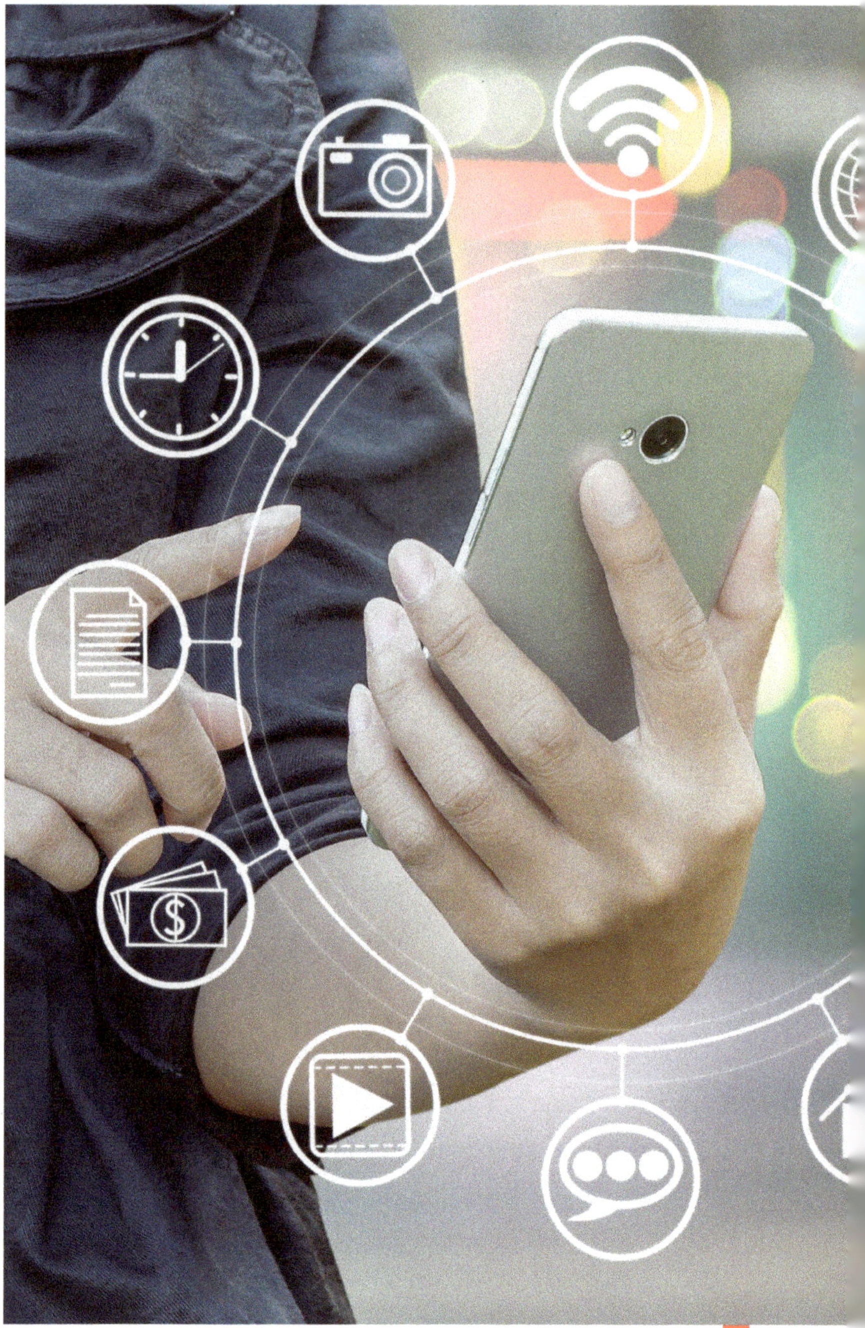

PART ONE
INVISIBLE TECH

Some technology is *actually invisible*. You can't see it or touch it at all. In fact, you wouldn't even know it was there if you didn't have a device to use it. Take the internet, for example. It plays such a massive role in our lives. We are constantly connected to it through our computers and phones and now even more random items like kitchen appliances and wristwatches. But have you ever actually *seen* the internet? Probably not, but the internet and invisible technology are with us everywhere we go. As we make modern advances in tech, our everyday devices are becoming lighter, faster, and more portable. We now have the flexibility and productivity that comes with a life without wires. In other words, we have the ability to take our books, movies, music, and much more with us on the go and add new content wherever we are at the touch of a button.

HOW DOES IT WORK?

How does invisible tech actually work? Let's dig into how some common invisible tech actually comes to life.

The Internet

Let's start with our trusty internet. Our devices wouldn't be as powerful without the internet, and many new innovations depend on a consistent internet connection. Even though the internet is invisible to us, it actually travels from place to place through super long cables under the ocean. It's true! The internet is actually just a network of computers that exchange **data**, or information, through underwater wires. When a computer makes a request for data from another computer, the information is sent piece by piece, not as a whole. These pieces of data are called **packets**, and they reassemble when they reach their destination to show you the image or text that you've requested. To understand how this works, imagine that you are looking at a completed puzzle. All of the pieces fit together perfectly, and you can see the image it creates clearly. But let's say you want to show the puzzle to a friend. When you send information from your computer to another computer online, it's kind of like the puzzle is broken up into its individual pieces, sent far away, and then reassembled at its destination (and all this happens extraordinarily fast). This process is called **packet switching**, and it helped the internet grow.

Did you know that the internet is actually made up of gigantic underwater cables that send data packets back and forth between computers? Sometimes sharks even bite through them! Remember that the next time your connection suddenly cuts out.

Mid-Century Text Messaging?

The internet as we know it today began in the 1950s and 1960s. Think back to the IBM computers at NASA's Langley Lab during this time. Computers were enormous, taking up almost as much space as the rooms they were in, and were programmed by hand. Though the computers (and people who programmed them) were becoming more powerful and accurate as time went on, they still worked in isolation. Was it possible for a computer to send information to another computer far away?

This was a question for a man named Joseph Licklider. He imagined what computers could do together, not just alone. He envisioned computers acting as what he called a "galactic network" that would allow people to research and communicate like never before. Building on his ideas, engineers who were funded by the United States Department of Defense Advanced Research Projects Agency (DARPA) sent the first online message in 1969.

BRB, Just Invented the Internet

The message was the word, LOGIN, but the computer crashed right after sending the *L* and *O* (an important reminder that some of the greatest feats in modern tech weren't instant successes). Engineers in the United States continued to experiment and develop the internet through the 1970s and 1980s, mostly on college campuses where research projects were often financed by the military. Finally, in the mid-1990s, the internet became available for widespread home use. You could pick up a free disc at a music or computer store, download the web-browsing software to your computer, and log on to the internet. By the 1990s, computers were much smaller and more affordable than earlier models, making the internet more widely accessible. The world was ready for the digital age.

Today, it's hard to imagine what life was life before the internet.

#TBT: A World Wide Web of Wires

When I was in middle school, I loved getting online. At that time, my computer's modem had to be connected to the telephone line in my parents' house. If I went online, they couldn't make or receive any phone calls. So, I had to carefully plan out what time I would be online. In addition, my blue iMac computer was a desktop model and sat on a table. I couldn't take it to my room or to the couch. In order to use the internet, I had to be in a specific place and only use it at specific times, which was fine at the time (mostly because we didn't have any other options). But portable tech would soon open up unlimited possibilities. The introduction of wireless technology allowed computers and devices to evolve in incredible ways. Instead of being wired, Wi-Fi allows the internet to be sent via a super high radio frequency that a device receives. The waves of the radio frequency travel millions of cycles per second, which provides a lightning-fast connection and gives us the flexibility to roam around our homes or schools while staying connected.

THE WI-FI MYSTIQUE

Fun fact: Some people believe Wi-Fi is an abbreviation of a longer term, wireless fidelity. As complex a role as Wi-Fi plays in our lives, its name is actually not short for anything. It turns out urban legends exist in invisible tech, too.

Bluetooth

The internet allows information to move from one computer to the next, and Wi-Fi gives us the freedom to move around while staying connected. But what if you want to connect devices that are not computers? Say, for instance, a speaker to play music from your phone? Sounds like a job for Bluetooth technology. Bluetooth can **pair**, or link, devices together, and it does this in a similar way to Wi-Fi. Bluetooth technology works on radio frequency and finds a common wave between two devices that are near each other. This allows the devices to link and communicate in a way that is efficient and does not require lots of battery power. How convenient is that?

When I'm alone, I like to listen to music on my headphones, so I pair my phone to them. But when I'm at a party, I want all of my friends to hear the music I'm playing, so I pair my phone to a speaker. Bluetooth makes quick, seamless, and wireless connection possible between devices. That includes pairing phones with car stereo systems that make hands-free calling and messaging safer for drivers. Very cool, right? But why is it called Bluetooth? The technology was actually named after Harald "Bluetooth" Gormsson, king of Denmark and Norway, who lived super long ago. King Bluetooth is credited with unifying Denmark; you might say he brought people together just like his namesake technology. Engineers even designed the Bluetooth symbol with inspiration from Viking inscriptions.

Cellular Technology

As the internet blossomed and the desire to be online around the clock grew stronger, cellular technology began to step up in a big way. Until the late 1990s, the telephone was a device connected to your home (like, physically wired into the wall). Each home had its own unique phone number, and your friends would call your house and ask whoever answered if they could talk to you. If you wanted some privacy, you would stretch the cord as far as it could go, which was most likely just as far as the next room. Though it wasn't that long ago, I can't imagine doing this today. Now I use my phone to navigate through the city, to help me with my work, and to watch viral videos of dogs. I have come to rely on having my phone with me at all times, which is mostly a good thing, but sometimes, I miss the days of hopping in the car with my family and listening to the radio—no distractions, just being in the moment.

It feels strange to even call my device a phone at this point, as it's the last thing I use it for.

Bluetooth

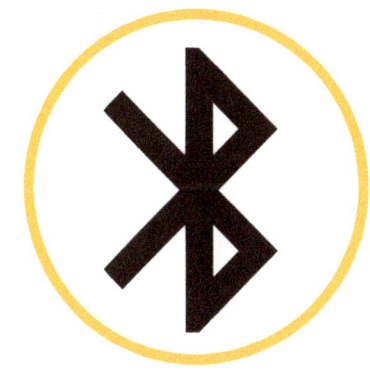

Bluetooth "pairs" devices, allowing them to work together. Connecting a phone to a car stereo or a headset is a great example of Bluetooth in action.

Cellular Technology

Not only can you make phone calls using cellular technology, but it's fast enough to stream a movie or build a world online.

Wi-Fi

In the early days of the internet you needed to plug your computer into the wall to get online. Today, Wi-Fi allows all kinds of devices to connect to a single internet connection.

Invisible Tech

It's a Bird, It's a Plane, It's a . . . Giant Cell Phone!

Cellular phones became popular in the late 1990s. If you watch television shows or movies from this time period, you'll see that they looked very different than they do today. They were huge black or gray brick-shaped devices with large antennas and big old buttons for dialing. If you had one during this time period, you were the definition of cool. It seems laughable now, but think about what a giant leap it was from talking on the phone in your parents' kitchen. It meant gaining a type of freedom that many people could never have imagined. When I look back at previous iterations of technology, I like to think about how much they improved on the inventions that came before. This is definitely the case with cellular phones. The first generation of cellular technology, called 1G phone service, allowed voice calls but often had spotty reception that wasn't very reliable. As the generations of service evolved from 1G to 4G, phones became more capable, adding the ability to send text messages, exchange data between callers, and provide mobile access to the internet. Mobile capability now approaches the fifth generation, 5G phone service, which promises to bring the fastest and most secure internet connection yet. How far can it go from here? I'm willing to bet that the future of mobile tech will blow our minds, just as it has been doing in the past 30 years.

Can you believe that all of these devices are cell phones? Big, small, flat, or flipped, each one helped inspire the phones we use today.

THE BIG BOOK OF INVISIBLE TECHNOLOGY

Invisible Tech

"Coder Says": Remix and Rewind!

Time: 15 minutes

The original idea: To help you understand how computers learn code, we'll use another person as our computer and program them using clear, descriptive commands. It's kind of like Simon Says because your computer has to do exactly what you program tells it to do. This is a great activity to help you start your coding journey.

CAUTION: Be sure you are instructing your partner to fill the glass with **cold water**; very hot water could burn their skin!

Materials

- A partner
- Index cards or scrap paper
- A pen, pencil, or marker
- A drinking glass

The Steps

1. Let's start with a program that will quench your partner's thirst—filling a glass of water! Take a moment to think through the actions or steps required to successfully fill a water glass.

2. Write down the steps to complete this task in a way that would make sense to anyone who reads them. Think critically about where your cups are stored and where the sink is in relation to them. You will have to carefully consider how you want your partner to complete this task. Start by walking through the steps on your own and writing down every action you take.

3. Next, read through the steps that you wrote. Did you start by telling your partner to walk to a cabinet? How will they know which direction to travel and where to reach? How should they turn the sink on and off? Is the faucet activated by a lever or a knob? How full should the cup be at the end of the program? Aim to write extremely specific directions so that your partner knows exactly what to do.

4. When you are ready, read your directions to your partner step-by-step. Were they able to successfully fill a glass? Chances are that they were not! Writing programs can be tricky, and it is expected that you will have to revise and try again. Take notes on any parts that were unclear, revise, and try again until you get it right!

Observations

Coding encourages us to think in different ways and problem solve, which makes our brains stronger. It forces us to think about how our directions will be interpreted, not just how to give them. If you ran into an error in your program, go back and think through how to fix it. Programmers have to get used to making mistakes and working through them, which is a big part of their job.

Modernize It

Now that you have the basic idea of coding, give it a try on a computer at your home, school, or library. If you're coding for the first time, you may want to use a block-based coding software like Scratch to get started (scratch.mit.edu). If you have some experience with Scratch and want to try something new, go to Code.org (https://code.org/) and learn from tutorials in HTML, CSS, JavaScript, and more. Learning how to code is an important skill you can teach yourself. Don't worry if you don't get it on the first couple of tries. It's important to stay persistent and flexible with your thinking as you learn.

The Hows & Whys

Knowing how code works on a very basic level will help you continue your journey in tech and build upon what you already know. Being a flexible thinker and finding ways to communicate clearly are two very valuable skills in tech.

Observations

Are there other simple tasks you could try the experiment with to practice thinking critically about action steps? "Programming" your partner to walk a square path or draw a smiling face are a few fun options to try.

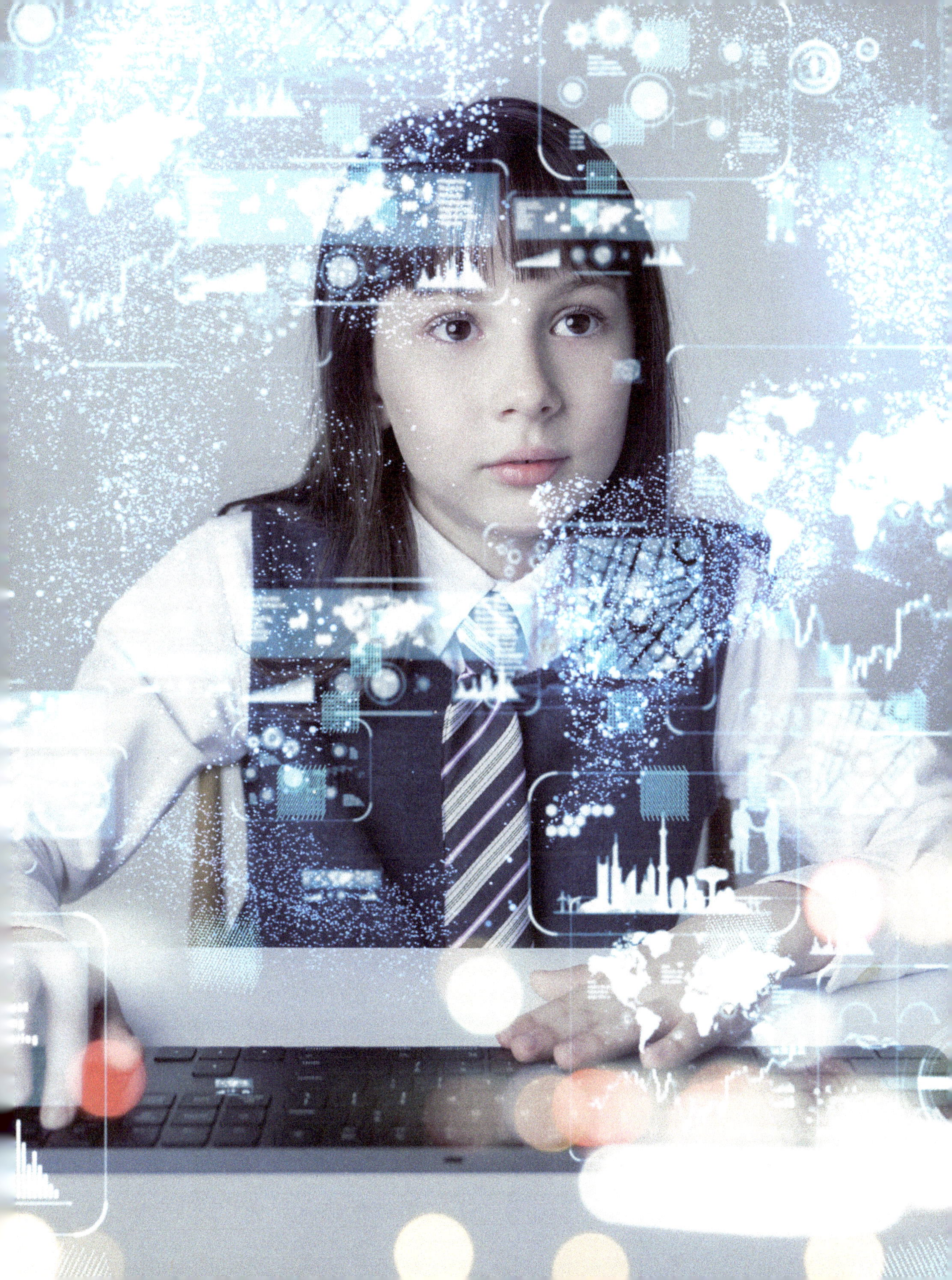

The Underwater Interweb

Time: 15 minutes

The original idea: As we learned on page 2, the internet travels from place to place through super long cables under the ocean. In this experiment, you'll test how quickly you can send data through your own set of cables. You can work with a partner or challenge yourself. How quickly do you think you can send your packet? Write down a guesstimate for how long it will take you to send and assemble your packet and test yourself against it. Were you faster or slower than you originally thought? Set another challenge with a more complex image and try again!

CAUTION: Be careful when you are using scissors. Hold them with the sharp point facing down and cover the sharp point with your closed hand while moving around the room or handing them to someone else.

Materials

- Crayons, markers, or colored pencils
- Letter size computer paper or construction paper
- Scissors
- Paper towel rolls (toilet paper or wrapping paper rolls will work, too)
- A timer
- Adhesive tape

The Steps

1. Line up three or four cardboard tubes in a row next to each other and use tape to hold them in place.
2. Draw a picture on a piece of paper using as many colors as you'd like. It can be a simple or complicated code, just don't show it to anyone. If you're having trouble thinking of something, draw a robot.
3. Fold your paper in half, and then in half once more. Carefully cut your picture into as many pieces as you are years old. Feel free to get creative with how you choose to cut the paper
4. Now, it's time to send your data. Start by setting your timer for the length of time you think it should take to distribute and reassemble your data. Crumple your cut-up pieces of data into small pieces and line them up in front of the tubes. You can flick them, throw them, or shoot them through. Use anything that works. Just make sure you do it quickly.
5. Rearrange your data on the other side of the tubes. How quickly could you or another person reassemble the original packet?

THE BIG BOOK OF INVISIBLE TECHNOLOGY

Observations

- What happened when you sent your data through the internet tubes? Did all of the pieces of your data make it to its destination?
- What was the biggest challenge you faced while sending and reassembling your data?
- How quickly do you think actual data travels through fiber-optic cables? Can you guess?

Modernize It

How quickly can you send information from one place to another? Can you do it in 30 seconds? How about 15 seconds? Think about how the lightning-fast internet has helped shape our society. What apps/tools/websites rely on instantaneous connection? What happens when a packet of information gets lost? What error messages have you seen on your devices?

The Hows & Whys

Think about a time when you had a super slow internet connection. What did you do to fix it? Challenge yourself to send information through the tubes several times until you can do it quickly. This process mimics how the internet has developed over time. Not too long ago, logging on to the internet took nearly a full minute, and now, it's almost instantaneous.

Observations

Why do you think that data is sent in packets instead of as a whole? What are some industries or occupations that rely on a consistent, quick internet connection?

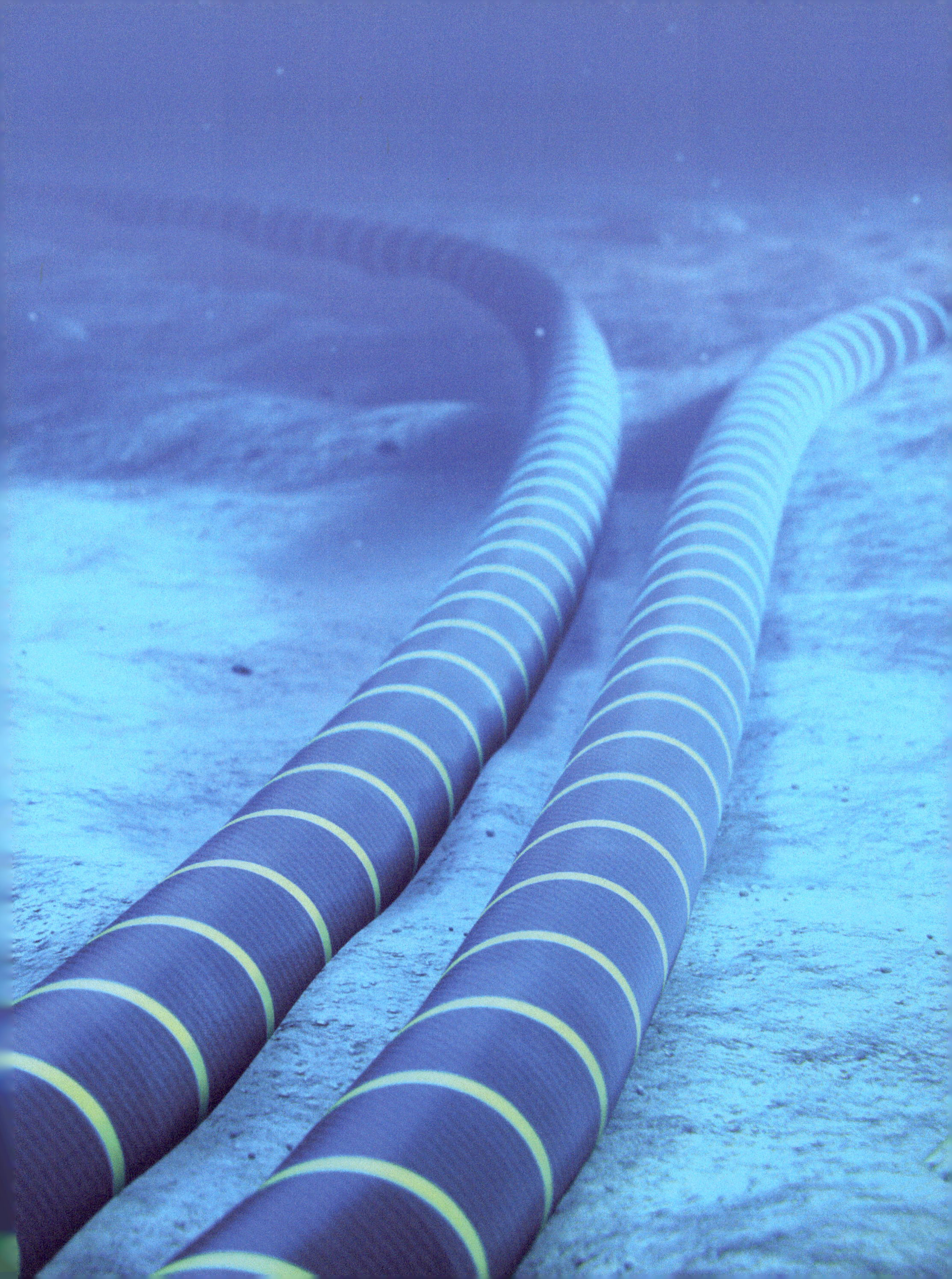

Machine Learning Madness

Time: 15 to 20 minutes

The original idea: Machine learning uses patterns and similarities to teach computers. Let's use materials that we already have to understand how machines learn to identify images and make decisions. For instance, how would you describe the common traits among dogs? You might write, "furry, tail, four legs." But how would you express it with images? Using magazines and newspapers, you'll find images that represent those traits. When your project is done, you'll grab a friend or parent to play a guessing game and see if someone can figure out what your image groupings represent.

CAUTION: Be careful when you are using scissors. Hold them with the sharp point facing down and cover the sharp point with your closed hand while moving around the room or handing them to someone else.

Materials

- Newspapers or magazines with pictures
- Scissors
- Scrap paper
- Markers
- A partner

The Steps

1. Start with the category of "nature". What images can you find that will fit this description? What do you consider to be a part of nature and what does not fit and why?

2. Look through old magazines and newspapers for images that represent each subject and its traits.

3. Cut out pictures that clearly show the people, animals, items, or concepts that you want to categorize.

4. Make a pile of five to ten images for each subject. If you're having difficulty finding enough images, use scratch paper to draw images that represent the traits you wrote down.

5. Gather your piles and explain to your partner that you want them to guess the subject you are trying to convey through images. Present your partner with each image in your pile, one at a time. At the end, they'll need to guess what it is.

Observations

- What kind of images were you able to find easily to represent your subjects?
- Were some subjects easier to represent in images than others? Did you make any images of your own?
- Did your partner have an easy or difficult time guessing what your images represented?

Modernize It

If you're ready to learn more about machine learning, you can start to train simple models online. IBM has a resource that will help you get started: www.ibm.org/activities/machine-learning-for-kids

The Hows & Whys

Although machine learning abilities are growing stronger, there can still be some major errors in the process. Consider the images that you chose and whether they are accurate for each category. What could go wrong if a machine did not correctly identify an image or category?

Observations

This exercise is fairly straightforward when you're identifying an animal or an item, but what about a concept, like "play" or "fun"? Challenge yourself to pick another concept and identify common traits—for instance "fun" could include images of smiles and laughter.

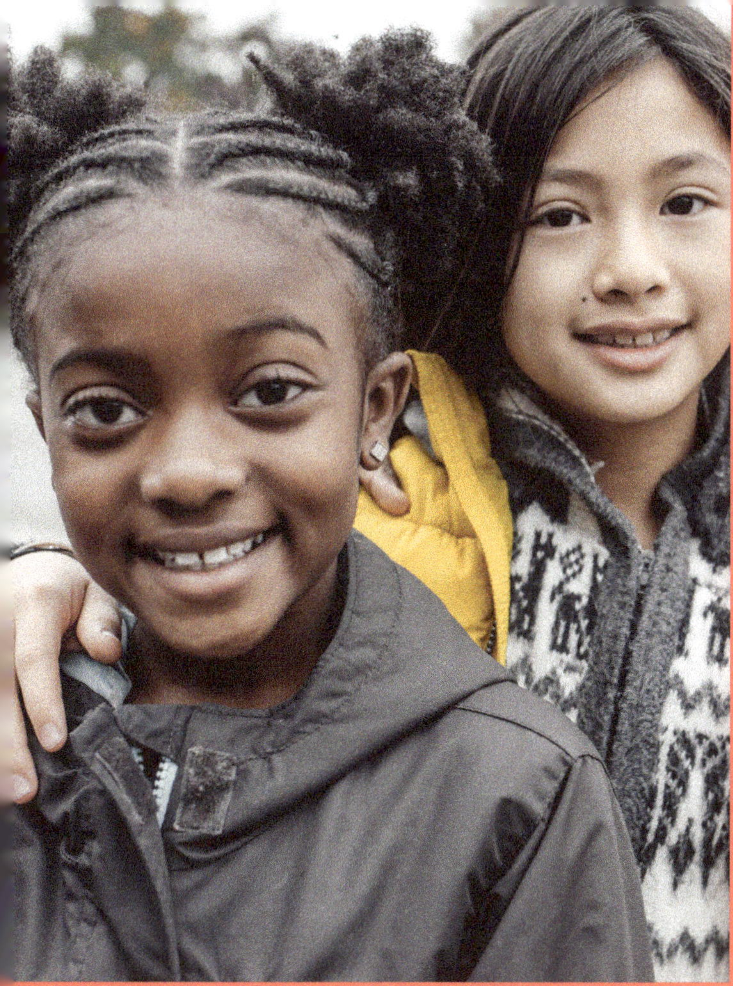
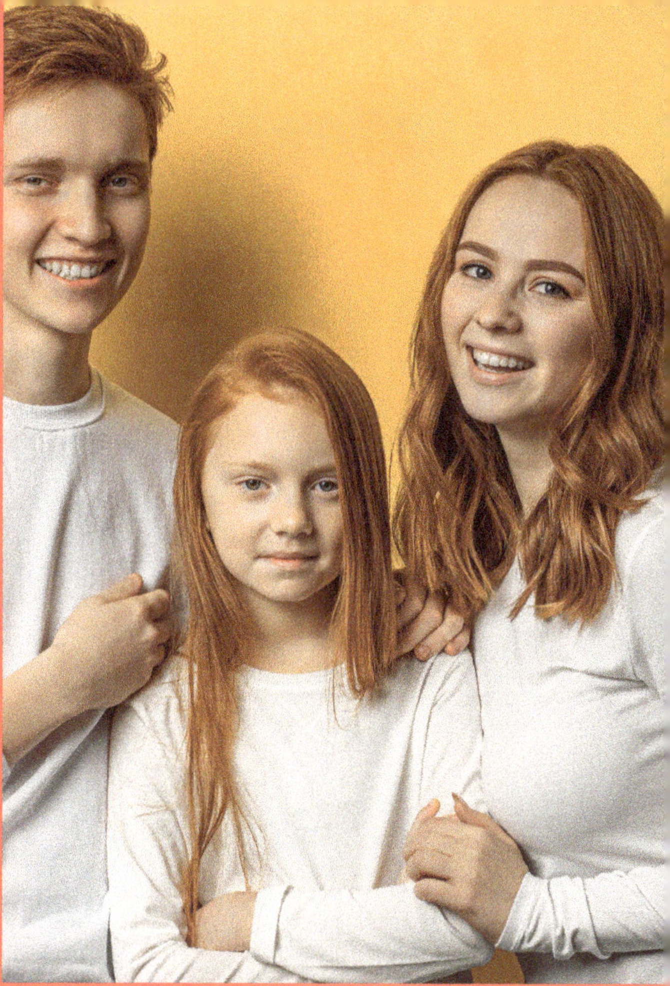
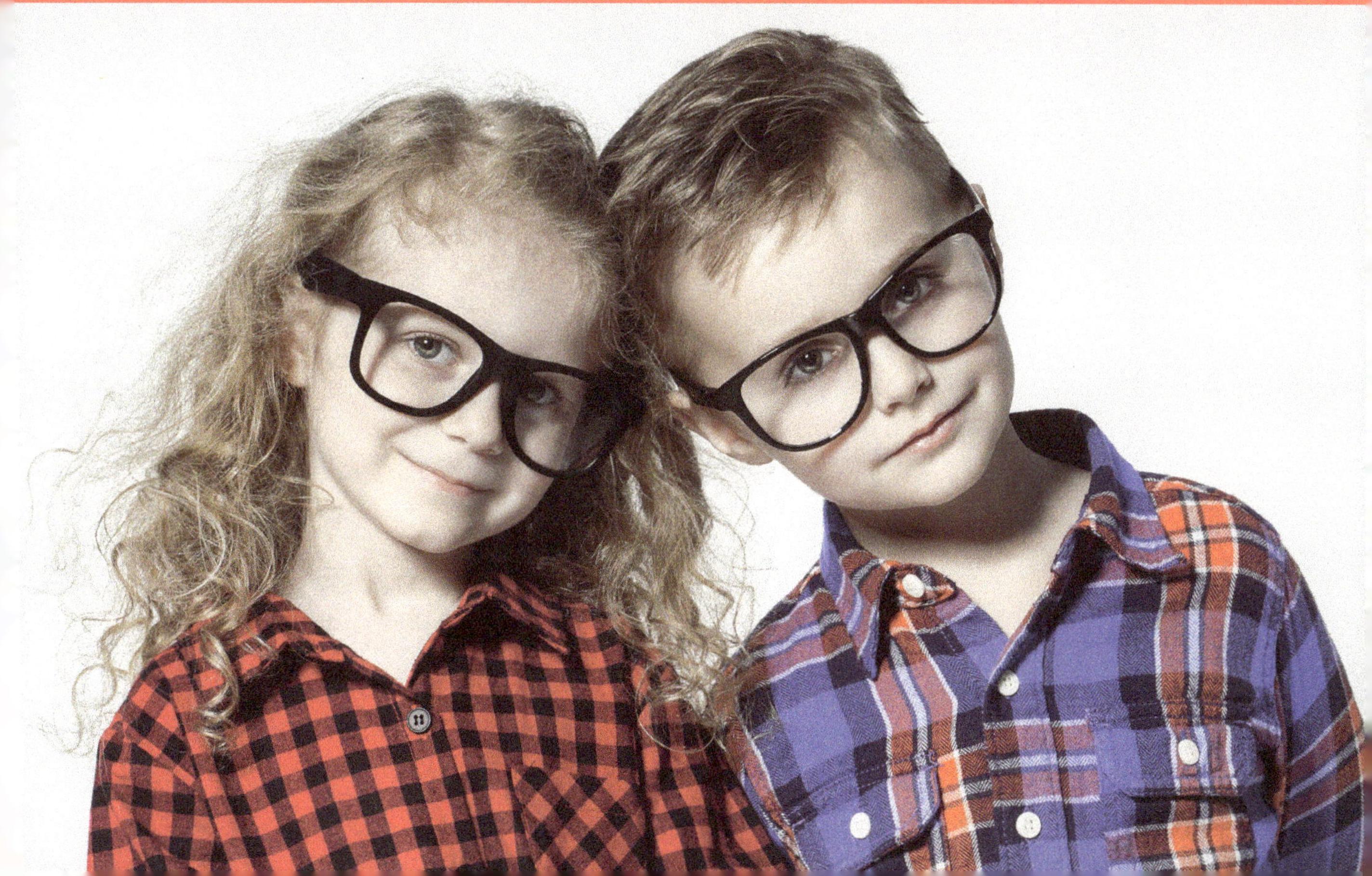

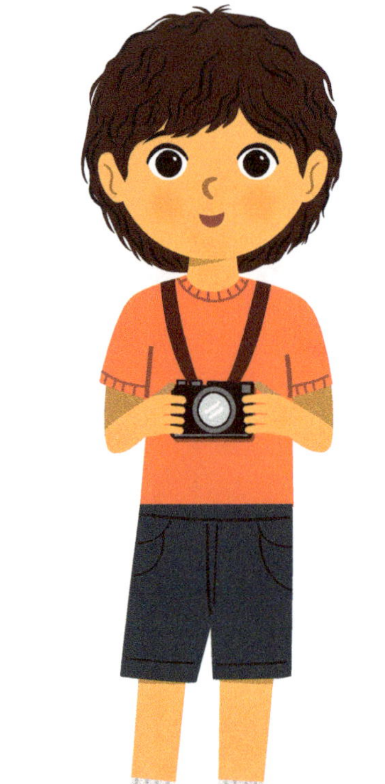

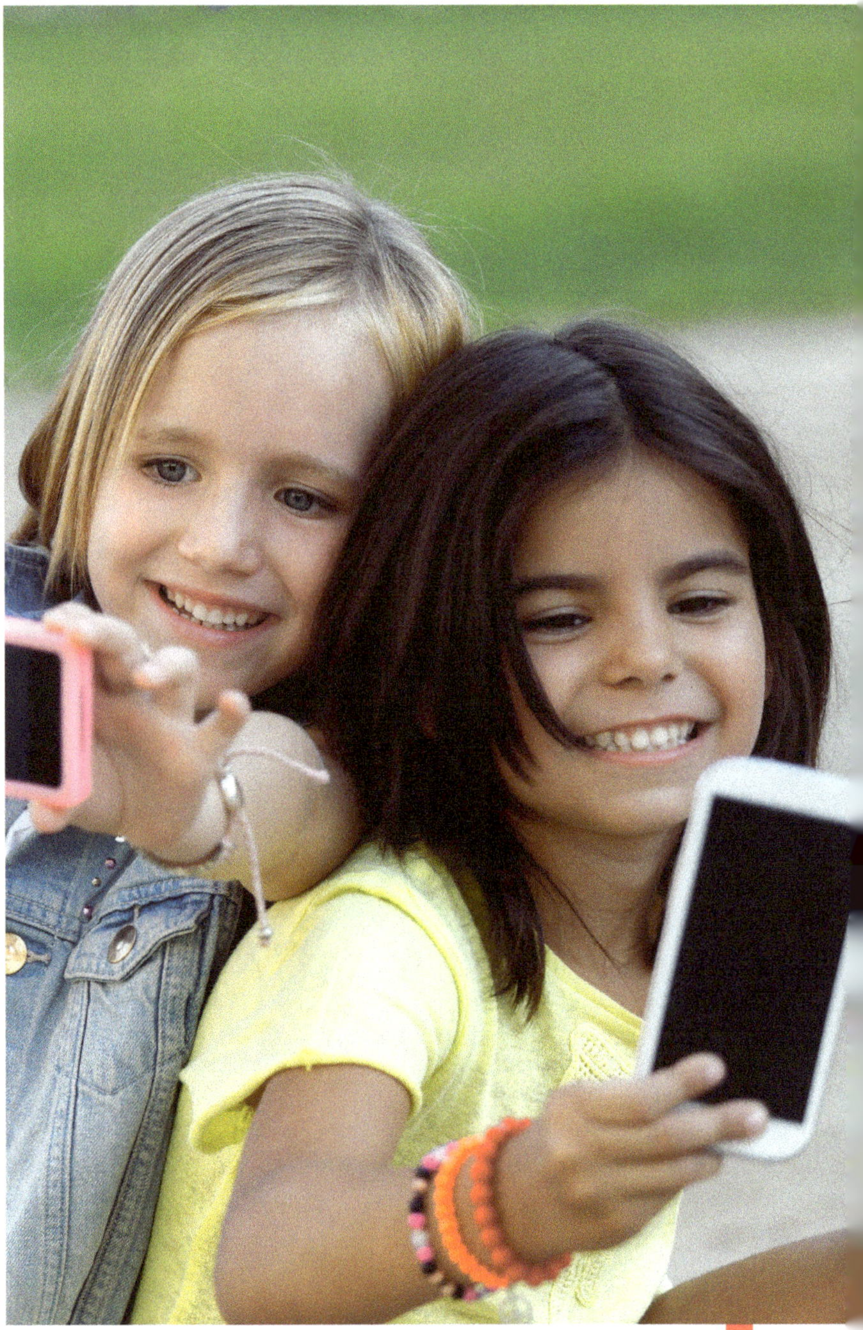

PART TWO
TECH YOU CAN TOUCH

Modern technology has made a huge impact on how we interact with the people and places around us. Now that we have discussed all kinds of invisible technology that powers our world, it's time to take a closer look at the tech you can actually touch. The invisible tech we learned about is a vital part of what powers all of the tech you can see and feel. Invisible tech, like Wi-Fi and Bluetooth, allows devices to run wirelessly, giving us more freedom to experiment with what machines are able to do now and in the future.

TECH IN OUR WORLD

Who Invented the First Robot?

The word *robot* entered our vocabulary in the 1920s from a word in Czech meaning forced labor. When computers first became popular in the 1960s, so did the curiosity of engineers who began to tinker with combinations of hardware and computer parts, creating robots as we know them. From 1963 to 1972, a team of engineers at the Stanford Research Institute began to work on a robot they called Shakey. Shakey was able to roll, spin, and move while following commands from its engineers. This was a major breakthrough in the history of robotics.

As the field of robotics progressed, so did the capabilities of the robots. Robots are now able to work, play, and interact with us like never before. We have even sent robots into outer space! Researchers like Dr. Ayanna Howard devote their work with robots to help make a difference in our world today. Dr. Howard has worked with robots for over 20 years at NASA and universities like Georgia Tech. In an interview with Google about her work, she says, "I believe that every engineer has a responsibility to make the world a better place. We are gifted with an amazing power to take people's wishes and make them a reality."

Dr. Ayanna Howard calls engineering "an amazing power to take people's wishes and make them a reality." What wish would you grant through robotics?

Robots

A **robot** is a machine that uses sensors to evaluate its environment, make decisions, and act. Robots run programs that allow them to move or act without someone controlling them in real time. The word we use to describe this attribute is **autonomous**, which means that they can operate independently without direct control from a human in the moment. Have you ever driven a remote-controlled toy car? If you have, you know that the car will not move unless you move it. You have to decide where it will go by steering it using the remote in your hands. If you see an obstacle in the way, *you* have to decide which movements will get your car around the obstacle. A robot is more sophisticated than a toy car, meaning that even though it may seem to have similar parts, it is able to run a program that has been written for it on its own. If that toy car was robotic, I wouldn't have to drive it because robots can make decisions based on the environment around them. Instead, I could watch the robot run the program I wrote for it. Maybe I would write some lines of code that prompt my robot to sense if there is an obstacle in the way and, if so, to move in the opposite direction.

Internet of Things and Smart Home Devices

We've discussed how the internet came to be and how people have come to rely on it in their daily lives. The internet has given us the ability to exchange information at lightning-fast speeds and stay connected to the rest of the world at all times. Now, we have taken this connection even further. In addition to our smartphones and computers connecting us to the Web, we now have **smart devices** in our homes, schools, workplaces, hospitals, and even gyms. Smart devices are part of what has been called the **Internet of Things (IOT)**. If a device is "smart," it generally means that it is connected to the internet and can send and receive information to other devices.

Drones

Another device that is changing how we work and live is the **drone**, called an Unmanned Aerial Vehicle (UAV) in the past. UAV refers to how drones operate: They fly **autonomously**, without direct control from a human, and their relatively small size and light weight allow them to maneuver in ways that larger airplanes cannot.

3D Printing

3D printing is the process of making an object in three dimensions from a digital file. There are a few different types of 3D printers. Some use plastic filament—Fused Deposition Modeling (FDM)—and others use a liquid called resin that is cured layer by layer with light—stereolithography (SLA). The term, 3D, refers to the first three dimensions: length, width, and height. In 3D printing, these are referred to as the X, Y, and Z **axes.**

Everyday Robots

When you think of a robot, what comes to mind? Is the robot you're picturing kind of human-like? Is it made of metal with a body that looks somewhat human? Does it speak in a monotone voice? Chances are you said yes to at least some of those questions because movies have greatly influenced how we think about and visualize robots in our world. In fact, some scary movies have influenced how people feel about robots becoming more prevalent in human life. Let's learn about what robots actually are so that we can think critically about them and consider their role in our lives both today and in the future. Movies, especially science fiction movies, spark our imagination but are only loosely based on fact (and sometimes have no factual basis at all). It's important that we learn about current science and technology so that we can separate real technological concepts from entertainment.

3D Printers

This 3D printer uses plastic filament to print objects like cups, replacement screws, even a prosthetic limb!

Drones

Drones can fly and navigate without humans on board.

Wearables

Wearable devices give us information about our health and activity levels. Some even let you make phone calls!

Tech You Can Touch

If It Looks Like a Duck and It Quacks Like a Duck, It Could Still Be a Robot

If you've ever seen an iRobot Roomba vacuum, you know that it runs a program that helps it clean carpets or hard floors. A Roomba is a good example of a working robot for us to learn from. The Roomba is a simple, disc-shaped robot with a hard outer shell and a few buttons on top. On the underside is the robot's **hardware**, or the physical parts of the robot that interact with the world. The program, or directions that it follows, is its **software**. The hardware and software work together to clean a room. The first Roomba robots ran a program called "random bounce." This meant that when the robot was powered on, the motors would power the wheels forward and the vacuum would start. When the robot's sensors detected an obstacle in the way, like a wall or sofa, the Roomba would bounce off of it and start cleaning in another direction. It would **loop**, or perform this repeated action many times until the entire room was clean. You can imagine that although the Roomba eventually vacuumed most of the room, it would take a long time, and some areas would be cleaned repeatedly while others were missed completely. As Roombas became more advanced, engineers were able to use better hardware and more effective programs to clean more efficiently. One way they did this was by adding more advanced sensors, tools that robots use to gather information about the world around them, which allowed them to detect stairs and map out the landscape of a room. If a robot needs to determine if a room is light or dark, it will use a light sensor to detect the condition of the room.

We often think that robots look like big metal humans, but they take on all kinds of shapes and sizes depending on their job.

When **roboticists**, robot designers, are designing a robot, they have to think about what its use will be and what sensors they'll need in order to collect information and make decisions. They also need to think about the robot's body, or hardware, that will make up its frame, motor, and power source. Most people tend to think of robots as **humanoids**, robots built in a human form. But the truth is that they come in all shapes and sizes. Some are massive, larger than a house, and others are smaller than a dime. Some have mechanical arms and wheels, and others are soft and fold like origami.

There is no rule about what a robot needs to look like; that decision is left to the creator. Many roboticists are inspired by nature when they design robots, especially in their movement. Some robots today are inspired by the flight of birds, the movement of fish, or other underwater creatures. Robots are becoming more common in our lives both at home and at work. But what about other devices in our homes like smart televisions, video doorbells, smart speakers, and wearable tech like smart watches? Are these robots, too?

Robotic Eyeballs

A question I'm often asked is, "Where are a robot's eyes?" Human eyeballs are powerful tools that can send all types of information to the brain, but robots do not see in the same ways that humans do. Remember, robots use sensors to gather information. If I walk down a street and see that a car is stopped about 25 feet away from me, I know that after checking the street sign, I can cross that street. Before a robot crosses a street, it may use its sensors to determine the distance and speed of a car that is approaching and make a decision about how to move based on this information. A robot does not need eyes to do this. (Although they are cuter with them!)

Robots use sensors as digital eyeballs: They can determine whether a room is light or dark or an object is near or far.

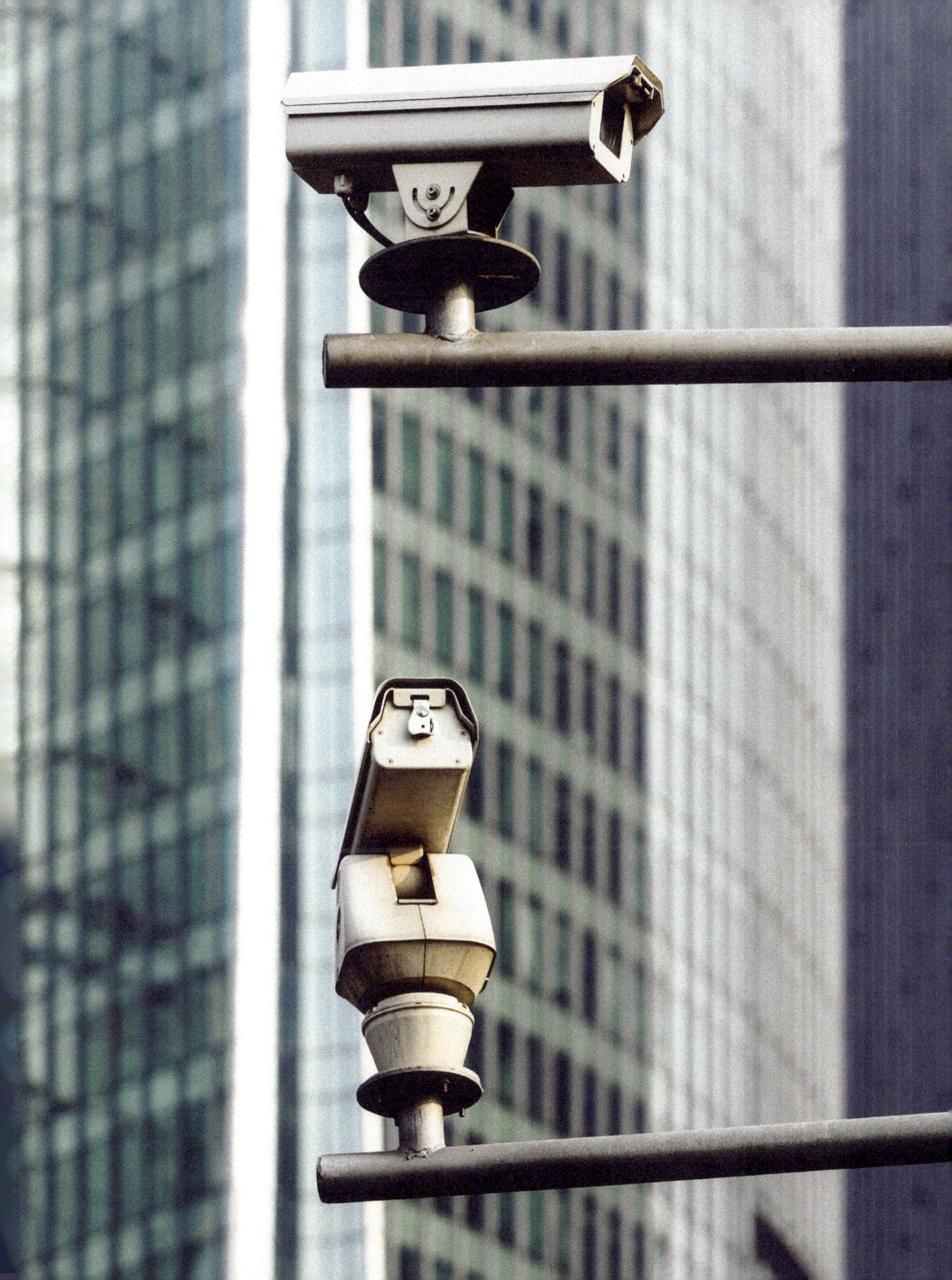

Making Sense of Sensors

Sensors are a very important part of robotics, so let's spend some time learning about what they can do. As humans, we use our five senses to gather information about our surroundings. Our skin, eyes, nose, mouth, and ears (among other systems) are powerful tools that help us sense and make decisions. I can use my eyes to gather visual information. If I see that the sun is up in the sky, I can open my curtains and let in natural light. If the moon is rising, it is now nighttime, and I know I need to turn on the lights in my home. Simple, right?

Laser Level

Want to hang a bunch of pictures in a row? A laser level will help you keep them straight.

No-Touch Thermometer

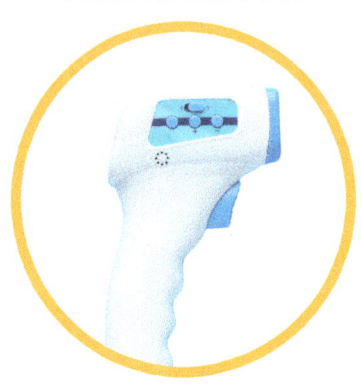

No-touch digital thermometers use heat sensors to measure a person's body temperature.

Digital Assistant

You don't need a TV remote to change the channel if your digital assistant's audio sensor is listening.

38 THE BIG BOOK OF INVISIBLE TECHNOLOGY

Goldilocks Could Have Gotten It Right the First Time

Another example is measuring temperature with our bodies. If I want to take a warm bath, I turn on a combination of hot and cold water and fill up the tub. When the tub is almost full, I cautiously stick my fingers in the water to determine how comfortable it is for my body. If it's too hot, I increase the cold water. If it's too cold, I add more hot water. I continue this process until the bath is just right for me. I don't actually know the temperature of the water when I get into it; I can only determine if it feels right for me. A robot with a temperature sensor would be able to measure how hot or cold the water is, and then adjust the temperature to an exact degree. Robots can be more precise in some ways. Imagine if I knew the perfect temperature of my bath water and could write a program to reheat the water to that exact degree. If the water began to cool, the sensors would record the change and the water could be heated to its original temperature. As a result, the bath could stay warm as long as I wanted. (Does this robotic bathtub already exist? If not, I need to start building it immediately!)

Some common examples of sensors that you'll find on robots are components that measure distance, sound, speed, and pressure. These sensors are especially important when robots are interacting with humans. Human interaction is a crucial part of robotic development. If a robot is programmed to give you a high five, it needs to be able to sense how much force it is going to apply to your hand and how quickly. You'd want it to make contact but not break your arm. Programming with accuracy is super important to ensure that people don't end up getting hurt, especially with more automated technology in transportation and health care.

Get Smart

Experts disagree about whether or not IOT and smart devices are considered robots. Smart devices have capabilities that their disconnected counterparts don't have.

Here's an example: I used to wash my clothes in a washing machine that would run when I put quarters in it. When I paid $1.25 in quarters, the machine would turn on, and I would pour laundry detergent over my clothes into the basin. I would choose the spin cycle that I needed, depending on how big the load was and how dirty the clothes were. After starting the cycle, I'd set my own timer for about 38 minutes, so I knew exactly when to come back and load my clothes into the dryer. This is how a standard washing machine still works today. However, a smart washing machine takes the process to another level. Smart washers have sensors that tell them how full the basin is and how dirty the clothes are. They can adjust their own settings based on this information and even send a notification to your phone when the cycle is over. Laundry is the chore that I like the least, so I'm looking forward to the day when the machine also folds the clothes and puts them away!

Though the smart washing machine is pretty cool, it isn't wildly different than doing the process with a traditional machine. Some IOT devices make a huge difference in daily life, and some not so much.

Wearables—IOT devices that you wear on your body, like the popular smart watch—collect information about a person's health, fitness, and sleep. Over time, they become more sophisticated and are able to do much more. Apple Watches, for instance, have saved numerous lives through their information-collecting sensors and ability to make calls and send messages. If an Apple Watch detects a hard fall over a far distance followed by a period of inactivity, it will dial 911 for emergency assistance and communicate the wearer's location via GPS. It can also detect an irregular heartbeat and send an alert that the user's vital signs have changed, prompting the user to see a doctor.

Smart devices can be used in very personal ways, including tracking people's movements during sleep and checking on newborn babies throughout the night. Although this technology is helpful, it collects a lot of data from its users and shares it with the companies that produce the devices. The sleep information of one person may not be that important, but when a company can gather information from thousands or even millions of people, it becomes valuable. As we generate more data and smart devices become more commonplace in our homes, we are trading our right to privacy for convenience and access to our tech wherever we go.

Continuous Glucose Monitor

People with diabetes can now monitor their blood sugar with their smart phone thanks to this wearable device that connects via Bluetooth."

Wireless Earbuds

No need to get all tied up in wires when you're working out; your headphones can talk to your device without them.

Smart Watch

Wondering how fast your heart is beating after that relay race? Your smart watch knows.

Tech You Can Touch

Eye in the Sky

Just like robots, drones run software and use mapping tools to figure out where they are supposed to go and what they're meant to do. They are powered by battery or fuel sources and have propellers that allow them to move vertically and horizontally into the sky.

Drones are used for many different purposes: photography, deliveries, surveillance, and military operations, among many others. Online retailers are always looking for fast and efficient ways to deliver packages, and drones may be the next step in delivery to your door. What benefits would drone delivery have in the future? Can you think of any drawbacks?

There's a lot of support for the use of drones in cities and other highly populated areas, but there is just as much pushback against this idea as some think they are an invasion of privacy. We also don't yet know how safe they will be in our existing living spaces, but with the increased needs for shipping and delivery, it seems that we will soon find out.

Drones are becoming increasingly common and can bring us almost anything, anywhere. But what if we could we make the things we need by ourselves using new 3D printing technology?

If you can dream it, you can print it.

All the 3D That's Fit to Print

You may have used a desktop printer to print from a computer before. With desktop printing, the machine takes exactly what is on your flat computer screen and prints the images or text onto a flat piece of paper using black or color ink. If I am going to write a school report about the ancient pyramids of Egypt, I may include an image of a pyramid along with my written report. A photograph of the pyramids is a 2D representation. I can't pick up or feel that pyramid on the paper because it has no depth.

A 3D printer works a bit differently. It allows me to create a pyramid that I can pick up and hold. How could I make a **replica**, or model, of what the real pyramids look like? There are many craft materials that I could use, but what if I wanted to be precise? FDM 3D printers work by stacking 3D models one thin level, or slice, at a time from the bottom to the very top of an object. The process is sometimes compared to a "robot arm controlling a hot glue gun."

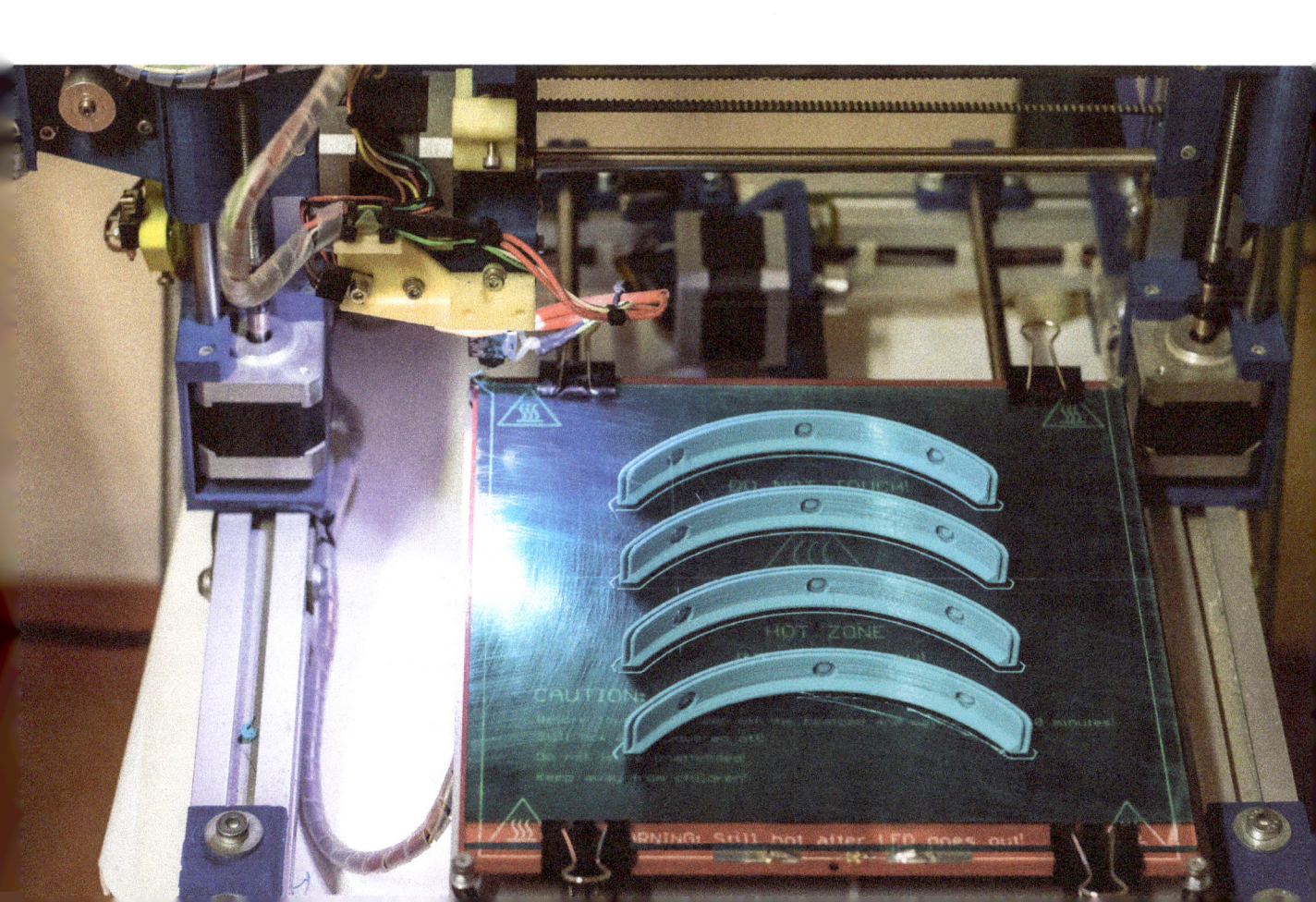

Fila-what?

Many 3D printers use a material called **filament**, which is made from plastic that's heated by the machine and cools in a precise pattern. If I were to 3D print a solid cube, my printer would start by tracing a very thin square of filament on the bottom of the print bed, and then move back and forth to fill in the empty space inside of it. As the filament cooled, it would provide a solid base to build another layer on top. It would then add another square layer and another on top of that until my cube is finished. Depending on what my file looked like, my 3D printer would follow the exact **path**, or program, needed to make the object I wanted.

FDM 3D Printer

FDM printers use plastic filament to build replicas from the bottom up.

3D Printer Filament

Printer filament comes in large spools and is often compared to the glue used in a hot glue gun.

Liquid 3D Printer

Rapid liquid printers don't use filament at all. They create 3D replicas using liquid resin and UV lasers.

THE BIG BOOK OF INVISIBLE TECHNOLOGY

How Does It Do That?

G-Code is the path that tells a machine how to move. It is the plan that's generated to make sure that an object is created successfully from start to finish. A 3D model is the computer file used to create the object. Just like when you print a page from a computer screen, a 3D model has specifications for what the object should look like when it's done.

Let's say, for example, that we wanted to 3D print a phone case. I always have a case on my iPhone to protect it from falls or accidental bumps and scratches. Because of this, the case needs to be made from a tough and durable material. Once I've decided that the plastic filament in my 3D printer would work well to make a new case, I'll need to find a 3D model of a case. I have two options: I can either download a model of an iPhone case from an online database, or I can measure my phone and design my own case using computer-aided design (CAD) software. Either way, I need to make sure the measurements are correct so that the case will snugly fit my phone. This is the part of the process where I can customize my phone case as well. Maybe I want to add my name to it or create a few cool designs. With CAD software, I can design or modify any file I'd like.

Using current 3D printers, it would take about one to two hours to print a case for my phone. It's amazing that I can design and create my own 3D items, but it is still a relatively slow process. However, 3D printing is quickly advancing, and great leaps in technology have allowed us to begin printing wearable items like clothes, jewelry, and shoes.

And it doesn't stop there. Remember that 3D printing is the process of building something in three dimensions, which means that liquids like cement and food can be 3D printed as well. In just a few short days, 3D printed homes could be created that are far less expensive than houses built the conventional way. Scientists are even experimenting with 3D printing artificial organs from human cells for transplants. What else do you think could be 3D printed?

Robots at Work

Many aspects of our lives have become automated. **Automation** means that a process is done automatically and often without human help. Robots are changing the way humans work in many ways. To understand what this could mean in the next 100 years, we first have to look back.

Let's start by thinking about the Industrial Revolution. The Industrial Revolution was a period of time during the nineteenth century when the use of machines became more widespread and revolutionized many industries, like farming, construction, and textiles. Instead of companies hiring people to work by hand, they were working in factories with equipment that was powered by coal and oil. Most of these jobs were dangerous, and people worked very long hours for little pay. The introduction of machinery made the work happen much faster, and business owners worked people beyond their limits, often until they were sick or injured, so that they could maximize their profits. Many children were employed during this era as well since child labor laws didn't yet exist. Factories were dangerous places for children to be in, let alone to work in, and they missed significant amounts of school, if they were able to go to school at all.

Many factory jobs weren't ideal for human bodies. So, it made sense that if machines helped humans work faster than by hand, couldn't they be even faster on their own? Enter the modern robot. Imagine that you're working in a factory and your job is to place a sticker on top of as many boxes as you can each day. Your day starts at 9 a.m. and ends at 5 p.m. It's important that a sticker makes it on top of each box before it is shipped out, so you do your best to do this quickly. How many stickers could you place each day? How about in a week or in a year? I would estimate that, at best, I could place about 500 stickers per day. I'd need a long lunch and lots of breaks during the day to rest my arm from all that work. But if I didn't sleep well the night before, or if I got distracted, I would probably place fewer than that. And if I got sick or hurt, I'd need to stay home from work, and that would be a day without any stickers, slowing down the factory process completely. Yikes! It doesn't seem like I would be a great candidate for this job at all!

It doesn't have a face or answer to its name, but this robot sure works hard!

Robots are perfect for this type of work because they have one job and one job only: the job you give to them. They don't eat lunch, they don't take breaks, and they don't sleep. If a robot malfunctions or needs to have a part replaced, it's usually much easier than when a person is injured and has to see a doctor to heal. Humans have rights and needs, and it is **ethical**, or the right thing, for someone to have work that pays fairly in a workplace where they are safe and respected. Robots (at least as they exist today) don't have those needs.

But Where's the Rest of It?

A lot of working robots are just arms. Yes, just arms. You might imagine a robot having a **humanoid** body, with a head, arms, and legs, but there is no need for the extra hardware in most manufacturing jobs. So, engineers just build robotic arms to complete the work. Thinking back to the sticker factory, it makes sense that a robot would replace me in that job. How many stickers do you think a robotic arm could place on top of a box in a day? Of course, there would be a lot of factors involved to figure out the answer to this question, like the speed of the robot's arm and how many boxes the factory produced, but I'd guess that a robotic arm would be 10 to 20 times faster than my own arm at the very least.

It makes sense to automate this job, but that would also mean I'd have to find another one. Some jobs can be done faster and more reliably by robots than humans. So, where does that leave us? What actually separates us from machines?

Robots today have automated lots of jobs and not just in factories. Robots have begun to take over industries that were traditionally human centered. The programs that robots run have become increasingly complex, and so has their hardware. Even industries that we may not have expected to be automated, like law and medicine, have benefitted from the use of robotics and **artificial intelligence (AI)**. AI is the ability for computers to think or learn from the information they're given.

We use artificial intelligence every day when we ask our devices to give us driving and walking directions.

East Road
Wood Road
Wild Street
First Street
Market Road
Site Road
Eagle Road
East Road
Green Street
A51
Eagle Road
Perimeter Road
West Street
A51
Broad Street

Reading, Writing, and Robotics

Technology has shifted the roles and responsibilities of people working in their respective fields. How will being a lawyer change if a machine can research thousands of court cases for you in seconds? How will being a surgeon change if robots can perform operations from inside a person's body? These are key questions to ask as the definition of work continues to change with the advancement of technology. Will humans even need to work at all after a certain point? What are the aspects of our work that *can't* be automated? And what will this mean for education?

The knowledge and skills needed to find a job are much different now than they were in the past. As students, it's important to think about *why* you learn what you do each day. With the evolution of technology, more knowledge is accessible via the internet than ever before. If we can retrieve any information we need at any point, then what skills should we learn?

Robots can take on some of human beings' most mundane tasks and free us up to do new things. The sky is the limit!

Digital Assistants

You Used to Have to Be a Movie Star to Have a Personal Assistant

One of the most popular devices in homes today are **digital assistants** found in smart speakers like Amazon's Alexa or Google Home. Digital assistants follow instructions we provide them using voice commands. They're also available in smartphones and computers like Siri from Apple or Cortana from Microsoft. These devices allow us to send and receive information with just our voices, but what happens on the other end? Who is actually responding? It's a good question to ask, and not enough people know the answer, even though the devices are becoming more and more popular.

Let's explore what's inside a virtual assistant—enabled device. Most of them are small and can sit comfortably on a desk or kitchen counter. They have a microphone and a speaker, so they can listen, record, and play back audio. There's also a small computer processor that connects the device to the internet and gives it Bluetooth capability.

Can You Hear Me Now?

Digital assistants are always listening to the sounds in a room in anticipation of hearing the word that will wake them. When a virtual assistant is called with a **wake word**—its name, for example—it'll light up to acknowledge that it has heard you. The light is a prompt for you to give a voice command. If you want to know what the weather will be for the day, you can ask, "What is the weather like today?" Instantly, your words are sent to the **cloud**, a place where digital information is stored but not on your device. The system determines that you want to hear what the weather is in your location and decides to play back the weather information gathered from its sources on the web.

Machine Learning and Artificial Intelligence

If you've ever used a digital assistant, you may have received a strange or incorrect response to your question or command. How do digital assistants find the right information?

Machines can learn, but they don't have to go to school to do so. They can be programmed to learn from experience. Simply put, machines can be trained to recognize patterns, similarities, and groups. Engineers train machines to recognize certain qualities so that they can make decisions on their own. If a machine identifies an image of a small furry creature with floppy ears, a wet nose, and waggly tail, it just may be a dog. But it would have to see lots of different images of many different types of dogs to give the right answer regularly.

Every time you ask your digital assistant a question, it is learning. Some are able to recognize your voice and address you by name.

Alexa, what's the weather like today?

It is cloudy with a chance of rain.

Tech You Can Touch

Robots Make Mistakes, Too

If engineers don't show the robot enough examples of something, the machine is more likely to make mistakes. For instance, they may think a super fluffy cat is a dog. It's important that engineers consider the information they give to machines and include wide and diverse examples so that machines can get it right. You may wonder why your digital device seems to get better at understanding you over time. You're not imagining things; it's called machine learning.

Invisible Robots!? Who's Driving That Car?!

Although cars have been around for quite some time now, modern advancements in automobile technology have changed our experience with them dramatically. From global positioning systems (GPS) to electric vehicles to automated driving, our relationship with car transportation is changing quite quickly.

When I learned to drive, my dad showed me all the important parts of the car and explained how crucial it was to be safe and alert on the road. He showed me how to pump gas and parallel park, which was the hardest part. Driving was fun and, at that time, there weren't many distractions in the car. I burned CDs with some of my favorite songs and was ready for the road.

Have you had this annoying experience? Rest assured that when it happens, your device is learning from the hiccup.

Today, my experience with cars is completely different. Because I live in a big city, I rarely have to drive. I can use my smartphone to track real-time train and bus schedules, and when I do take a car, I use a ride-share app to find one. The ride-share app process is simple: I use a map to identify where I am and where I want to go, and I am matched with a driver. When I get into the car, I am able to see the route I will take and how long it takes to get there with the current traffic.

Tools like GPS and mobile data allow me to plan ahead for my daily travel, although I am still almost always late (sorry). Technology is a big part of my daily commute, but I still ride in cars driven by people. Lots of people, especially in big cities, find work through driving or in the navigation and delivery industries. Let's examine the pros and cons of cars and trucks driven by drivers versus automated systems.

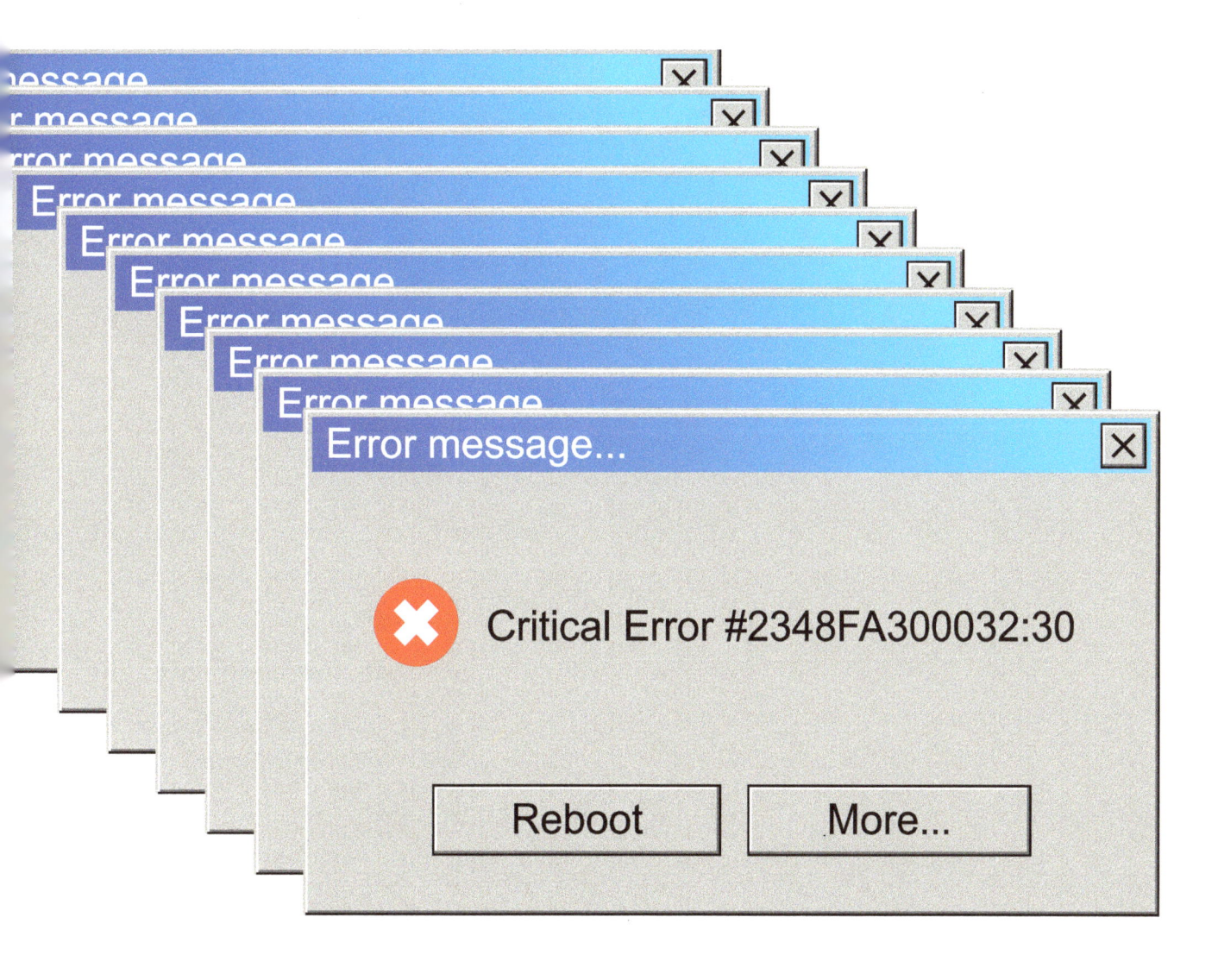

LIDAR: An All-Seeing Eye?

Automated cars use a system called Light Detection and Ranging (LIDAR) to see. Here is how it works: The LIDAR system consists of a laser, scanner, and GPS, and it can be seen spinning on top of the roof of an autonomous car driving down the street. The laser can detect distances by sending pulses of light out to the objects around it while measuring how long it takes for the pulses to return. In other words, it can see what is around it in real time and make decisions based on that information. LIDAR is important because it can detect even small or slight objects in its path, like a tricycle that may be in the road. LIDAR is helping automated cars advance and evolve, but it's not perfect and still causes accidents that could have been prevented by a human driver.

Light Detection and Ranging (LIDAR) is the technology that allows driverless cars to "see" what is on the road around them.

GPS

Your devices use GPS to figure out where you are in the world, and how to get where you're going. LIDAR uses it to do the same.

Laser Pointer

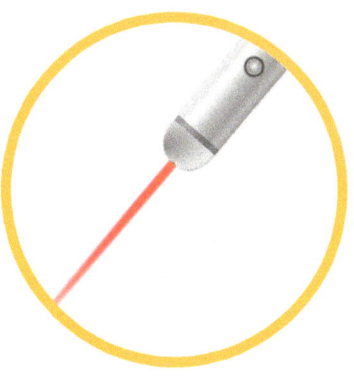

When LIDAR's lasers detect another object, it knows how far away it is.

Image Scanner

A digital scanner can make a perfect copy of a photograph, article, or any visual information you may want to save to your hard drive, not unlike LIDAR.

Computer Creativity

Visual art is a very important part of our human experience. It lets us express our thoughts and emotions through a creative outlet and allows other people to connect with what we feel. Visual art is found in every culture's history and takes on the essence of the people that create it.

Technology has helped art evolve in new and exciting ways. In addition to traditional mediums that are still used, like painting, sculpture, and photography, technology has given us new digital tools to express ourselves. Photography was once extremely expensive and painstaking, which meant that only some people in a society, usually only the wealthy, were photographed. Now, digital photography is much more accessible through the use of smartphones that can both snap and share images in seconds. Digital photography gives people from diverse backgrounds access to advanced tools to document their world. Some artists have even created movies using the cameras on their phones. Imagine how many more people can express their artistic vision by having these tools.

Artists can use technology to combine physical and digital mediums and push the boundaries of their work.

A Whole New World

Art takes on a new dimension with a little help from modern tech. **Virtual reality (VR)** uses computer technology to create a simulated environment, usually experienced through a headset display. VR allows the user to explore distant places through immersive photography and sensory experiences. Virtual environments can also be created through 3D art. Instead of painting on paper, VR allows artists to paint in 3D space: up, down, and all around them. Think about how creating and experiencing art will change using this technology.

Augmented reality (AR) brings the virtual and real worlds together. When looking through a smartphone or tablet camera, the user can see virtual objects in real spaces. For example, AR can allow you to see the size and shape of a framed painting on a living room wall before you purchase it. AR uses sensors to measure the size and shape of digital elements and their real surroundings. Both VR and AR have opened up new possibilities for artists and allowed the experience of digital art to become more sensory.

Digital art has also helped the evolution and enjoyment of video games. What was once a pixelated 2D experience has become a completely immersive and digitally stunning visual experience. Game development is an exciting field, and 3D artists are introducing new techniques experimenting with texture, lighting, and color. Video games combine storytelling and art in a special way, and they are only getting started. As art evolves, what other technology do you think will influence artists?

Want to take a walk with the dinosaurs? Augmented reality can make it happen.

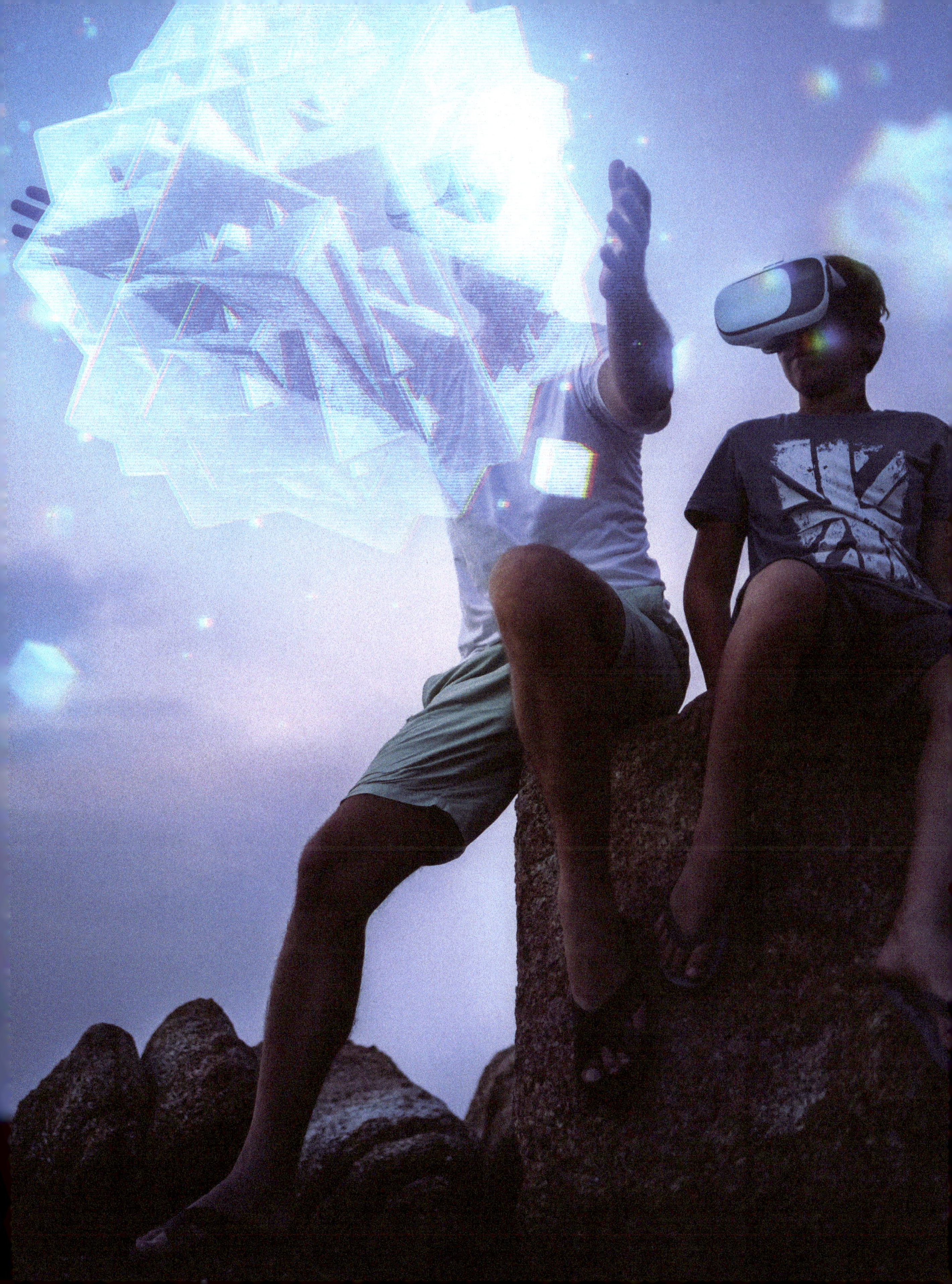

Animal Robo-Bodies!

Time: 20 minutes

The original idea: When you think of robots, you most likely think of metal, circuits, and screws. But did you know that a lot of robots have been inspired by nature? Roboticists study how different animals move, swim, grab, and jump to gain inspiration for their own machines. This is called **biomimetics**. There are robots that have been inspired by snakes, ostriches, cheetahs, and even cockroaches. Let's think about animals you know and the traits they possess that we could mimic in our machines.

CAUTION: Be careful when you are using scissors. Hold them with the sharp point facing down and cover the sharp point with your closed hand while moving around the room or handing them to someone else.

Materials
- Yarn
- Construction paper or heavy recycled paper
- Scissors
- Paper towel rolls or cardboard
- Adhesive tape
- Straws (thin and thick sizes)

The Steps

1. Let's build a snake together! Think about the ways a snake can move and start sketching some different sizes, shapes, and lengths of snakes to get some ideas for your robo-body.

2. For an easy snake shape, you can use a paper towel roll or a few toilet paper rolls cut into pieces. You can decide how many "joints," or separate pieces you want your snake to have. Place your pieces end-to-end.

3. Punch a hole at both ends of each piece and tie them together with a short piece of yarn.

4. Attach one long piece of yarn to the head of your snake so you can lead it around! What about this shape and movement would make a good robot body? How many different ways can it move?

THE BIG BOOK OF INVISIBLE TECHNOLOGY

5. Gently pull the yarn cord to see if your animal moves at its joints. This activity mimics robotic movement, moving one or multiple parts of the hardware at a time.

Observations

- Were you able to make your animal move?
- Which animal movements were the easiest to mimic?
- Which were the most difficult animal movements to mimic?

Modernize It

Use a computer at home or at your local library to access Scratch (scratch.mit.edu/) and experiment with movement blocks or lines of code to mimic an animal of your choice.

The Hows & Whys

Technology and nature are very different, but they can inspire one another. What other parts of nature can inspire your creativity in tech?

Project link for reference

www.instructables.com/id/Robotic-Hand-Science-Project/

Observations

> *Try this experiment with other animals! Make a short list of a few creatures you find interesting, listing some of their features and the interesting ways they can move. Choose an animal from your list that could inspire your project and give your robot a competitive edge.*

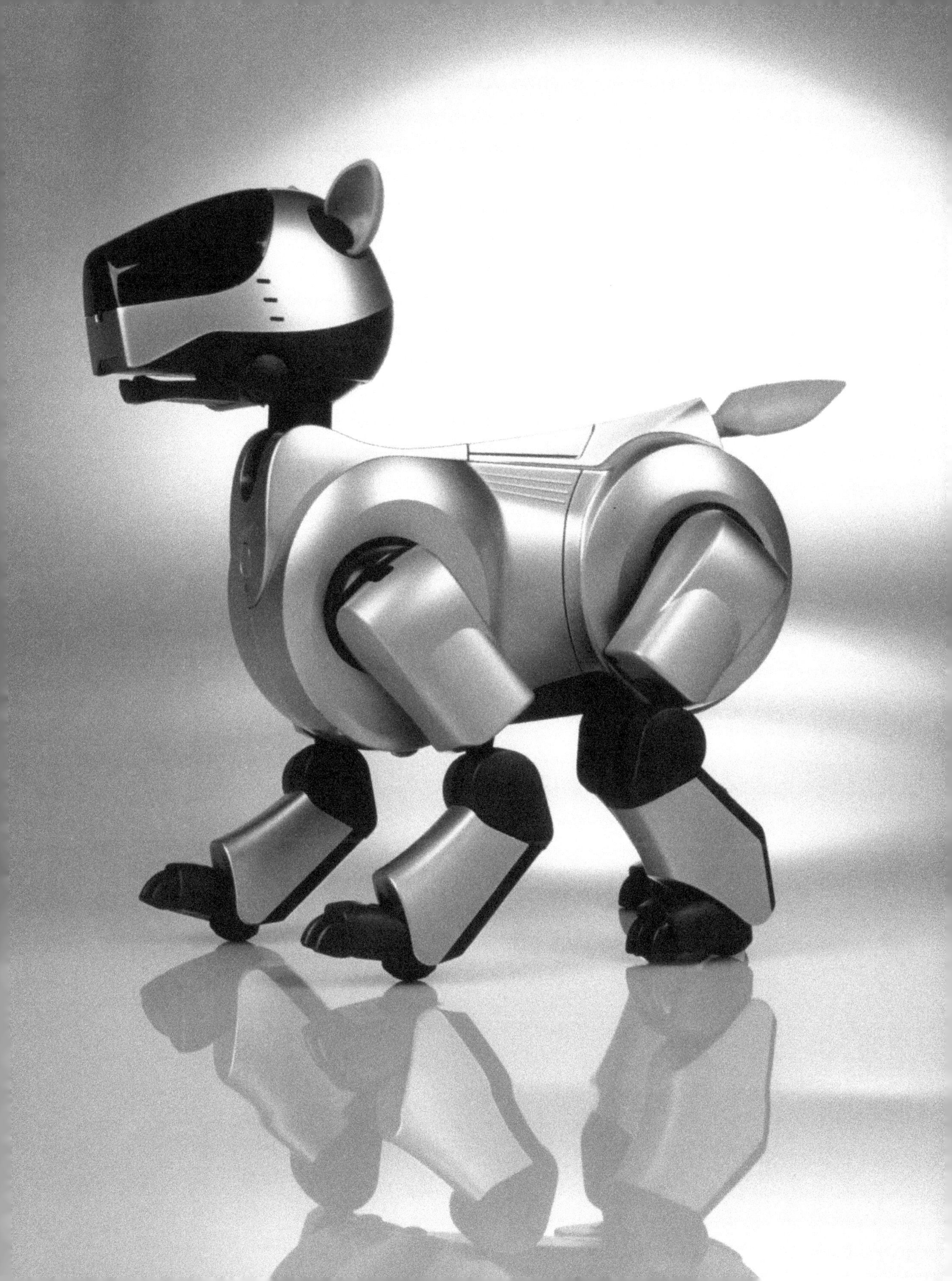

A Little Bit Like LIDAR

Time: 20 minutes

The original idea: LIDAR (Light Detection and Ranging) is the technology used to operate autonomous vehicles like drones and driverless cars. Let's get creative with texture and light and explore how this works.

CAUTION: Ask for permission to use the materials for this project. If you choose to use papier-mâché with your model, ask a grown-up for help.

Materials

- Paper of various textures (tissue paper, construction paper, corrugated cardboard, felt, aluminum foil, etc.)
- Poster board
- Newspaper
- Crayons or markers
- Liquid glue
- Glue stick
- Bottle caps
- Corks
- Cardboard tubes
- Ruler
- Scissors
- Toy car
- Papier-mâché paste (a 1:1 ratio of liquid glue and water)
- Flashlight

The Steps

1. Sketch out a road map for your toy car to travel on using a large poster board. You can get as creative as you'd like with planning the route. Try drawing your route to scale. You may add water, pedestrians, greenery, anything you'd like.

2. Robotic vehicles use sensors to determine the surfaces they should travel on. Decide which textures are okay for your car to drive on and which should make it stop. For instance, it's okay for my car to drive on newspaper or aluminum foil because those materials represent roads and bridges. But my car should avoid hitting corks, which represent obstacles like other cars or people in the road.

3. After planning out your design, start to create your texture map from recycled materials around your home. Using a small flashlight, experiment by shining it on the textured surfaces that you've created. The flashlight represents the LIDAR's laser, which is able to "see" by measuring height and distances between the car and the objects around it.

4. Finish your texture map and play with how your car navigates through it. Could you drive your car with your eyes closed? What helps you navigate without seeing?

Observations
- Which of your senses are helping you navigate your car over the map?
- Can you navigate with the lights off in a dark room? With just a flashlight?
- How do you think autonomous vehicles learn how to drive in new places? How do places become familiar to them?

Modernize It

If you have access to a robotics kit at school, try experimenting with an **ultrasonic sensor** to measure distance. This sensor uses ultrasonic sound waves to figure out its position relative to other objects. If your school doesn't have an ultrasonic sensor, ask your teacher if a local high school or college would allow you to visit their science department and use theirs. Also, ask your teacher if you can do some experiments that measure distance and motion to learn more about this topic.

The Hows & Whys

Transportation is rapidly changing. It won't be long before you're picked up by a robot and whisked off to your destination. What are the pros and cons of autonomous vehicles on our roads and in our skies?

Link for reference

www.geospatialworld.net/blogs/what-is-lidar-technology-and-how-does-it-work/

Observations

Can you think of other everyday objects or technologies that could use LIDAR to automate?

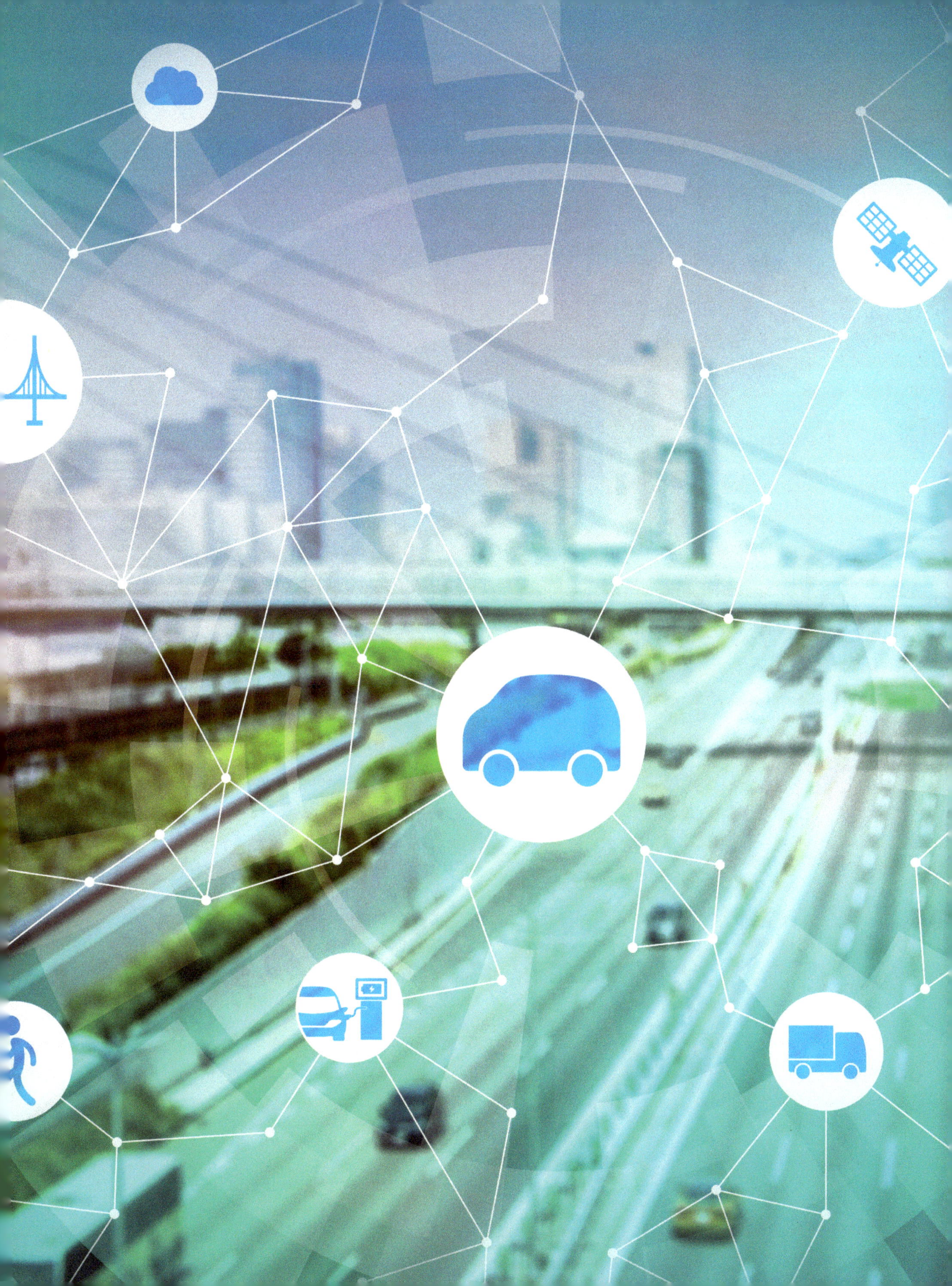

Stack Exchange

Time: 15 minutes

The original idea: A 3D print can take on almost any shape you could possibly imagine. To help you understand how the 3D printing process works, we're going to play with this concept and make 3D shapes using clay. Like a 3D printer, we will use the clay to build a simple design, layer by layer. Don't worry about what your model looks like in the end, just have fun making it. The process is more valuable than the product.

CAUTION: Carefully use a dull plastic knife to cut shapes or make textures in the clay.

Materials

- Modeling clay
- Plastic knife
- Plastic or paper cup
- Plastic containers of various shapes and sizes
- Cookie cutters
- Paper
- Pen or pencil

The Steps

1. Begin by making about 20 long, thin ropes of clay. Roll them out under your palm and make each one about six inches long.

2. Create the base of your 3D design by drawing a 2D shape on a piece of paper. If you aren't sure what shape to draw, start with a heart or a square with rounded edges.

3. Take your first rope and lay it on top of the shape that you drew. Repeat the process over and over, building the clay layers to get some vertical height. This is how a 3D printer builds from the bottom to the top.

4. Feel free to get creative and change your design or alternate the position of the layers as you build upward.

5. Once you complete your design, try building another way by using a cup, container, or cookie cutter to cut out several dozen shapes of the same design. Stack the thin layers of your design atop one another to replicate the 3D printing process.

Observations

What kind of everyday objects could people design and make themselves if everyone had a 3D printer in their home?

Modernize It

Find out if your school or local library has a 3D printer you could use to create your own 3D models.

The Hows & Whys

Consumers can use 3D printing to make their own products at home with just a few clicks of a mouse. With easy-to-use design tools and less expensive machines, we can make our own toys, tools, art, and so much more.

Observations

_____
_____
_____
_____
_____
_____
_____
_____
_____
_____
_____
_____
_____
_____

> *The use of 3D printing is changing many industries, like construction, food preparation and service, medicine, and fashion. How do you think 3D printing could have a positive impact on the way we live today?*

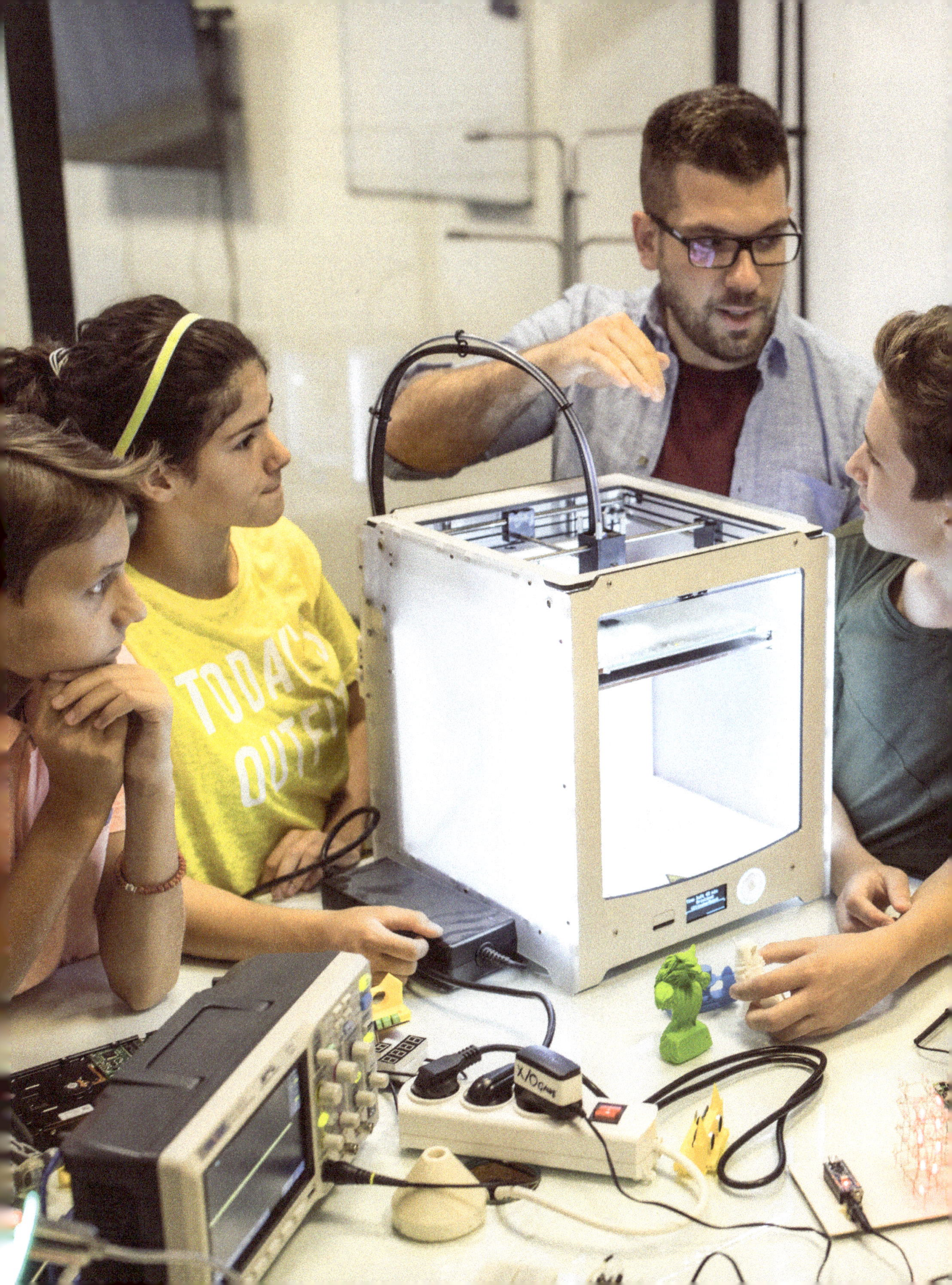

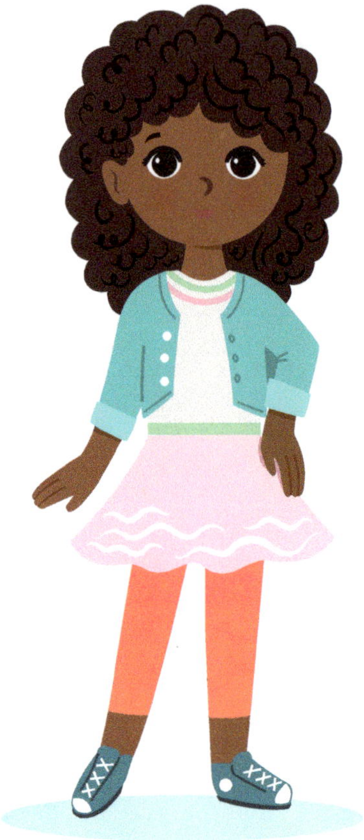
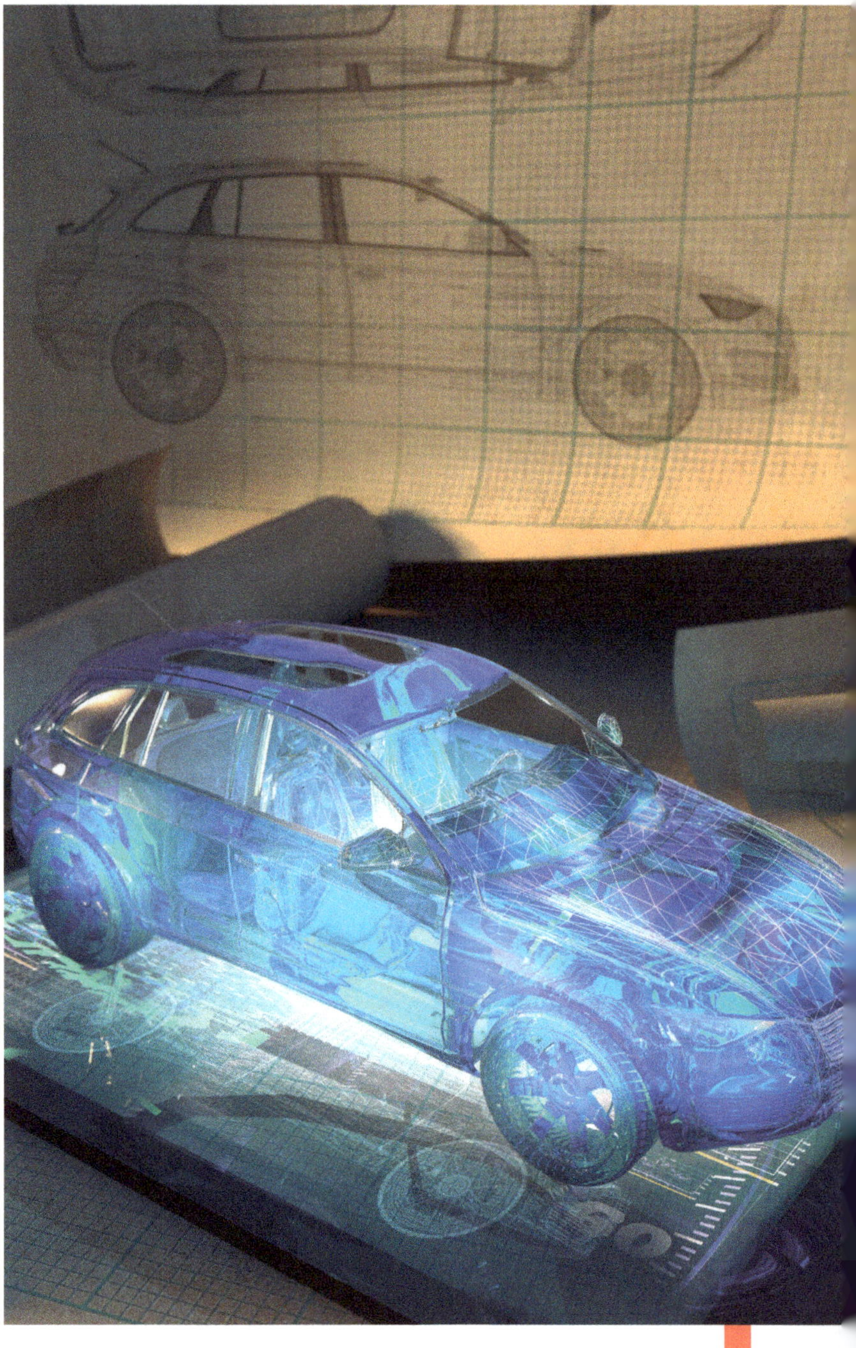

PART THREE
TECH TO THE FUTURE

After learning about the amazing tech around us, how do you feel? Curious? Inspired? Skeptical? A lot of the technology that we've learned about is very new to our world, which means that we don't exactly know what long-term effects it will have on our bodies, our environment, and the way that we interact with each other. In the long span of human history, the technology covered in this book is just a blip on the timeline. But because it's so powerful, it gives us a unique opportunity to change our existence like never before.

We've spent time thinking about lots of tech, both seen and unseen, and now it's time to think critically about how we can make visible and valuable changes in our world and for our future. It's important to take a close look at yourself, your life, and your world. The world is a complex place. Even though there's a lot of creativity, invention, and technological progress, there are also major problems that negatively affect people, animals, and our environment. Now that you have gained knowledge that will help you innovate, or introduce something new to the world, what will you create? It's time to use your imagination to dream up unique and extraordinary ideas. Let's get the process started by thinking about some of the tech you already use and innovations that would further change life for the better.

THINK ABOUT IT!

One of the best ways to innovate is to brainstorm about your own life, needs, and wants. Allow yourself to dream and let go of any limits that you're putting on your ideas. Many groundbreaking inventors were criticized and laughed at for their revolutionary ideas. But that creativity and bravery help us evolve. The world needs each and every one of your ideas to make it a better place. Let's get started!

Making an Innovation Plan

Start your innovation plan by thinking about the tech that you use frequently and the purpose it fulfills. Then, think about how it could be made even better in the future. I picked a few devices that I use and thought about why they are so significant to me.

EXISTING TECHNOLOGY	PURPOSE	POSSIBILITY
Smartphone	Instant connection with family and friends	Teleportation ability?
Laptop Computer	Productivity for work, sharing ideas and files	Ability to share textures or tastes? How about smells?
Smart Watch	Health and fitness tracking, hands-free use of phone	Can it be any smaller or more seamless? More integrated into my skin?
3D Printer	Creating 3D objects from digital files	Can we print living things? Can I clone myself through 3D printing?

Next, I took some time to think about new possibilities for the tech I already use. It's okay that I don't know exactly how these ideas will work—having an idea is the first step. By making a chart, you can keep track of the ideas you have, and then research which technology will help you make your vision a reality. I think it would be incredible to 3D print a clone of myself, so I will continue to learn about 3D printing and start to do more research about printing with living cells. How does that even work? What have scientists been able to do so far, and where is it heading?

I want to take my idea even further. A lot of tech is just for fun or entertainment, and that's great. But it's important that we also think about how innovation can make the world a better place. My 3D printing idea could be used to create a clone of myself that I could trick people with, sending it to early morning meetings and letting me sleep in. That sounds amazing. But how could I use that same idea to make the world a better place? What if 3D printing live cells could help people who are sick and need organ replacements or have been injured and need to heal their skin or bones? This application of my idea would be a major medical breakthrough and could help so many people.

Get creative and list as many possibilities as you can in your innovation plan. If you feel comfortable, share your plan with a friend or a grown-up, and have a discussion about technology in the future. You may also want to keep track of your ideas in a journal and add sketches or photographs that inspire you to accompany your plans.

Our Changing World

You may already know that using technology comes with a lot of responsibility and that it can be used to help or hurt the people around us. Living a digital life means that our money, photos, and private information exists online and can be accessed by people who shouldn't see it. Because life on the web is evolving so quickly, the laws haven't been able to keep up with it. Unfortunately, that can make the internet an unsafe place. Here are a few tips to remember to make sure you are safe online:

- If you create new accounts or download new apps, make sure that a grown-up knows that you're using them. Don't post pictures of yourself, your location, or your school without first getting permission from a parent or trusted guardian. You can also tell them whether or not you feel comfortable with your picture being posted on their accounts as well.

- A lot of information that looks or seems real on the internet is not. You may see an interesting article from a website you've never heard of and share it with friends. But just because it's online doesn't make it factual. This happens a lot, even to adults, and these fake stories have the power to influence your opinion based on inaccurate or faulty information.

- Stay alert! If someone sends you a message that makes you feel uncomfortable or unsafe, tell a grown-up about it immediately. You don't have to keep it a secret.

- You may feel pressure to follow accounts or channels that are popular, but you don't have to. Your experience online is for you to enjoy, which means you don't have to watch or follow anyone who doesn't make you feel good.

- Be careful when you're shopping online or exchanging money digitally. Make sure that the right amount is going to the right place. Take care to keep your usernames, passwords, and account information private.

- You can share your account passwords with a grown-up, but don't share your passwords with friends. Just as you wouldn't hand out keys to your front door, your accounts are more likely to remain secure if fewer people have your passwords.

- There's so much amazing content available online, and we love to share what we find. But it's very important that we respect the **intellectual property (IP)** of others—creative works like photographs, drawings, films, and music—and only share something if we're given permission first. The internet is not a free-for-all. Would you ever copy your friend's paper at school? Of course not. In the same way, you can't take whatever you see on Google and assume it's free for you to use.

> *Ultimately, we have the responsibility to make sure that we are using technology ethically and meaningfully. The laws will eventually begin to change to protect internet users, but it will happen slowly. Until then it's up to us to be good internet citizens, using tech for good, and staying safe while doing so.*

Tech to the Future

Building Healthy Habits

There are so many ways to immerse ourselves in tech these days. Whether it is streaming a show, playing video games, checking apps, or some other digital distraction, you may find your eyes are glued to a screen for most of the day. It's true that technology expands our world by giving us access to information from far and wide, but what about the people and places near to us? Are we missing out on quality time with family and friends? How about making time to interact with nature?

As humans, we're a part of the natural world and are meant to enjoy it. Spending time outdoors and taking in clean air and sunshine is good for our bodies and minds. I really love being outside and enjoying activities with friends. Unfortunately, I often feel an urge to check my phone when I'm with them and have to remind myself not to get distracted. This is becoming harder to do because tech companies design their products to be engaging on purpose, meaning that it'll be harder for you to put them down. Whether it's starting a new video before your current one ends or sending you bright red notifications throughout the day, they want your attention! Whenever you feel an urge to check your phone or tablet, or if you know you need a break from a game you can't put down, try the following steps:

- Take a deep breath in through your nose and slowly let it out through your mouth. Breathe as deeply as you can.

- Close your eyes for about five seconds.

- Ask yourself, "Why do I want to use my computer/tablet/phone/device right now?" Is it because you are bored? Maybe feeling nervous or shy in a social environment? Are you lonely and want to connect with friends or family? Understanding the reason why you want to use your device is very important.

Don't get lost behind your screen—the real world can inspire your best inventions!

- Try to make a choice that will make you feel good. If you're bored, find a good book to read. Feeling nervous? Set a goal to speak to just one person before you reach for your phone.

Remember that your devices are great tools, but they shouldn't hold you back. As our lives become more digital, we'll have to make intentional choices to be living well with our tech.

TECHNICALLY CONVENIENT

Some tech is for fun and convenience. In fact, *a lot* of it is these days. Companies have created thousands of items to keep us entertained with tech that has no other purpose. However, breakthroughs in technology have the power to be so much more! Some organizations have used tech for good, helping alleviate modern problems.

For example, LifeNabled is an organization that makes prosthetic arms and legs for children in Guatemala who have been injured. Traditionally, it's extremely expensive to get a prosthetic limb, and children's bodies grow and change rapidly, meaning that they would need to be replaced frequently. LifeNabled 3D scans each child's body and 3D prints a prosthetic that will fit them comfortably. The process is much less expensive and allows the children feel confident and capable. This is an amazing way to use 3D printing. Can you think of another way that you could use technology for good?

A custom prosthetic leg is formed by an FDM 3D printer.

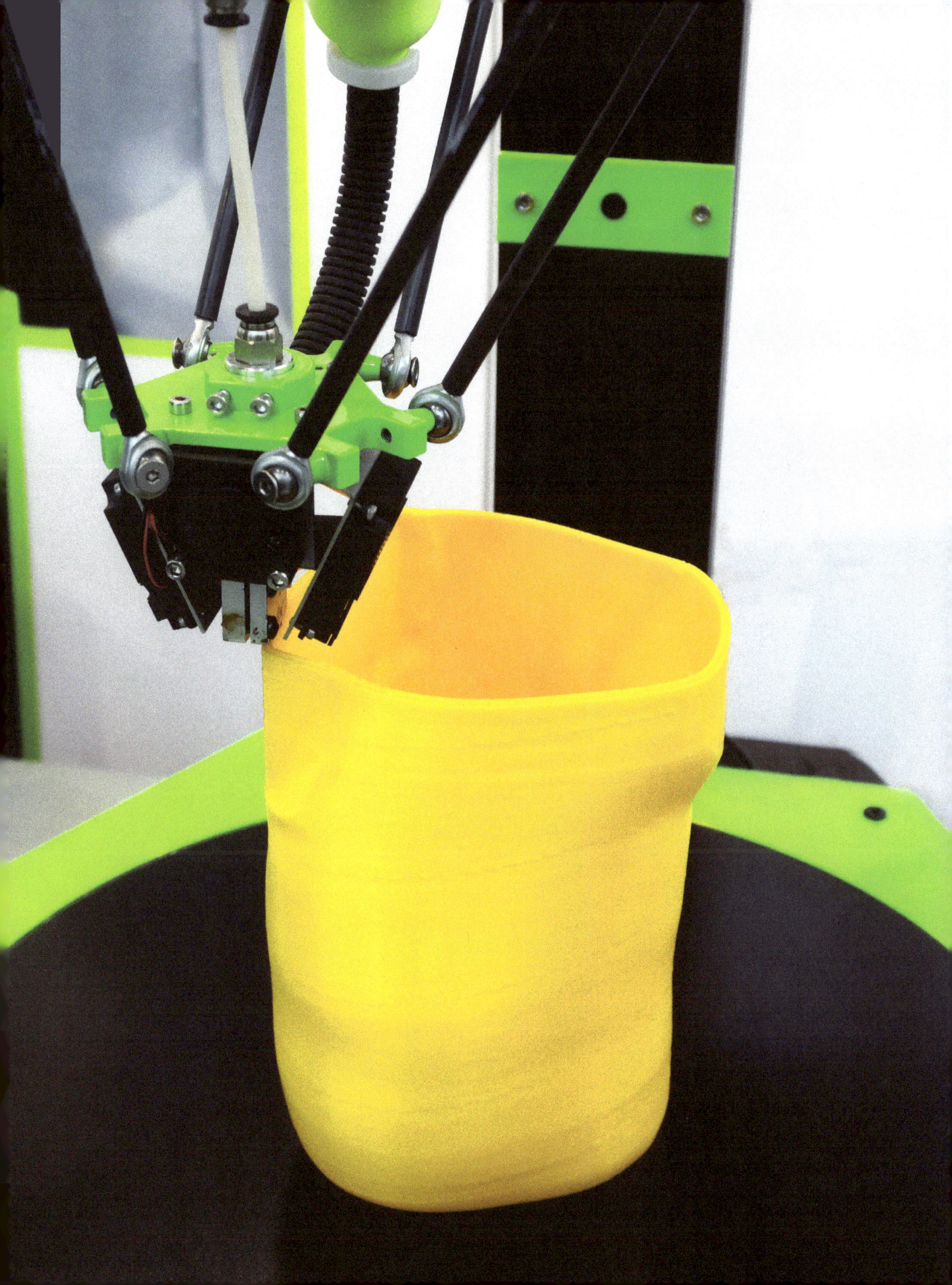

It's Your Turn!

Maybe you've been thinking about a problem in your school or neighborhood and want to come up with a way to solve it. Whether it's big or small, one way to get started on an idea is to use **design thinking**. Design thinking is a way to approach a problem through thinking about it deeply and specifically. It's actually used by companies and organizations looking to solve problems, and you can use the same process, too. We will face new challenges as time goes on, and it's important that we have a way to find solutions. As technology changes the nature of our lives, design thinking will help us find potential solutions to problems in a fast and focused way.

Let's learn about each step of the process.

- **Empathize:** The first step is to think about an issue that affects you or your community. Let's use an example from a school community. My school wants to be more environmentally friendly, but there are lots of ways that teachers and students are creating waste. I need to empathize, or understand and share the feelings that people in the community have, so I'll spend time interviewing them about excessive waste in school and looking at the issue from their point of view. They may tell me that there is trash left around the building and the garden and that lots of recyclables end up in the trash can. Other students may have concerns about the amount of paper that's being printed and thrown away after they finish an assignment. I would interview as many people as I could about this topic so that I could get the most information.

- **Define:** Now that I've done my research, I need to define, or explain, what the issue actually is. Because many of the responses were about unnecessary waste going in the trash can, I can define the problem by stating: "The school has an issue with excess waste going into the trash/landfill that could have been recycled or eliminated completely."

- **Ideate:** This step is all about the brainstorm. Now, it's time to come up with creative solutions that'll help solve your problem. One of my interviewees told me that she sees plastic spoons, knives, and forks in the trash cans all the time. Students eat breakfast, lunch, and an afterschool snack at school, so they could be wasting up to nine utensils per day. How can we eliminate this waste? Well, one solution could be that each student has their own set of reusable utensils. These could even include chopsticks and straws. There is a big sink in the cafeteria, so students could wash their silverware after they've finished eating. In the ideation stage, I'll start to sketch out my idea. Maybe I start to sketch a reusable utensil set and case that has a fork, knife, spoon, and chopsticks in it. I show my plans to some of the people that I interviewed, and they like my idea. In fact, they give me some valuable feedback. They let me know that I could combine the fork and spoon to make a spork, which would make room for a straw in the kit.

- **Prototype:** In the prototype phase, I'm going to make a simple model of my idea that I can share. Because I now know that 3D printing can be used to make objects come to life, I'm going to take my sketches and draw them using a CAD program like Tinkercad. I am going to make a few different shapes and sizes of my meal kit to see what my users would prefer. I'm also going to start choosing materials both for my utensils and the case that it would be carried in. I wonder if fabric would work well? This is the time to experiment.

- **Test:** Now, it's time to roll out my idea with a few friends who are willing to test, or try, my prototype. In this case, I have three friends use their meal kit for a day, and then get their constructive feedback about how it went. **Constructive feedback** is so valuable because it gives very specific and helpful information about what works and what doesn't. They may not find it as useful as I originally expected it to be, and that's okay! My goal is to make something that'll solve a problem and not create a new one. Try to use the constructive feedback that you get to improve your design. My users wanted a case that could be easily washed in the sink, so I've changed my fabric case to one made of a vinyl material.

And that's it! I've created something that could help reduce the waste problem in my school. I may have to do some of the steps over and over to make sure that I'm finding a good solution that people will use. You can use the exact same steps to work through a problem in your community. Get started by making a short list and try it out.

The Future Is for You

Now that you've read all about where we've been as a society and where we are going, I want you to know something very significant. The future is for YOU to design. Yes, *you*! Your ideas matter. Your concerns matter. Your experiences and voice matter, too. The world needs your imagination to solve its toughest problems, and it can't happen without *you*.

In many places around the world, including the United States, access to education is still denied to many people. Your education is important, and you are in charge of it. Education is more than just going to school. It's also what you learn from the world around you and the people who you know. Yes, going to school will teach you a lot, but learning from another person, possibly even a mentor or role model, is a valuable experience as well.

I hope this book has inspired you and that you'll continue on your journey using tech in awesome ways. I truly believe that the key to a better world lies in using technology meaningfully and ethically. I know there's good in the world because you are here. The key to moving forward together is inside of you, ready to shine, and I can't wait to see it.

What will you code, invent, or create, to bring positive change to our world?

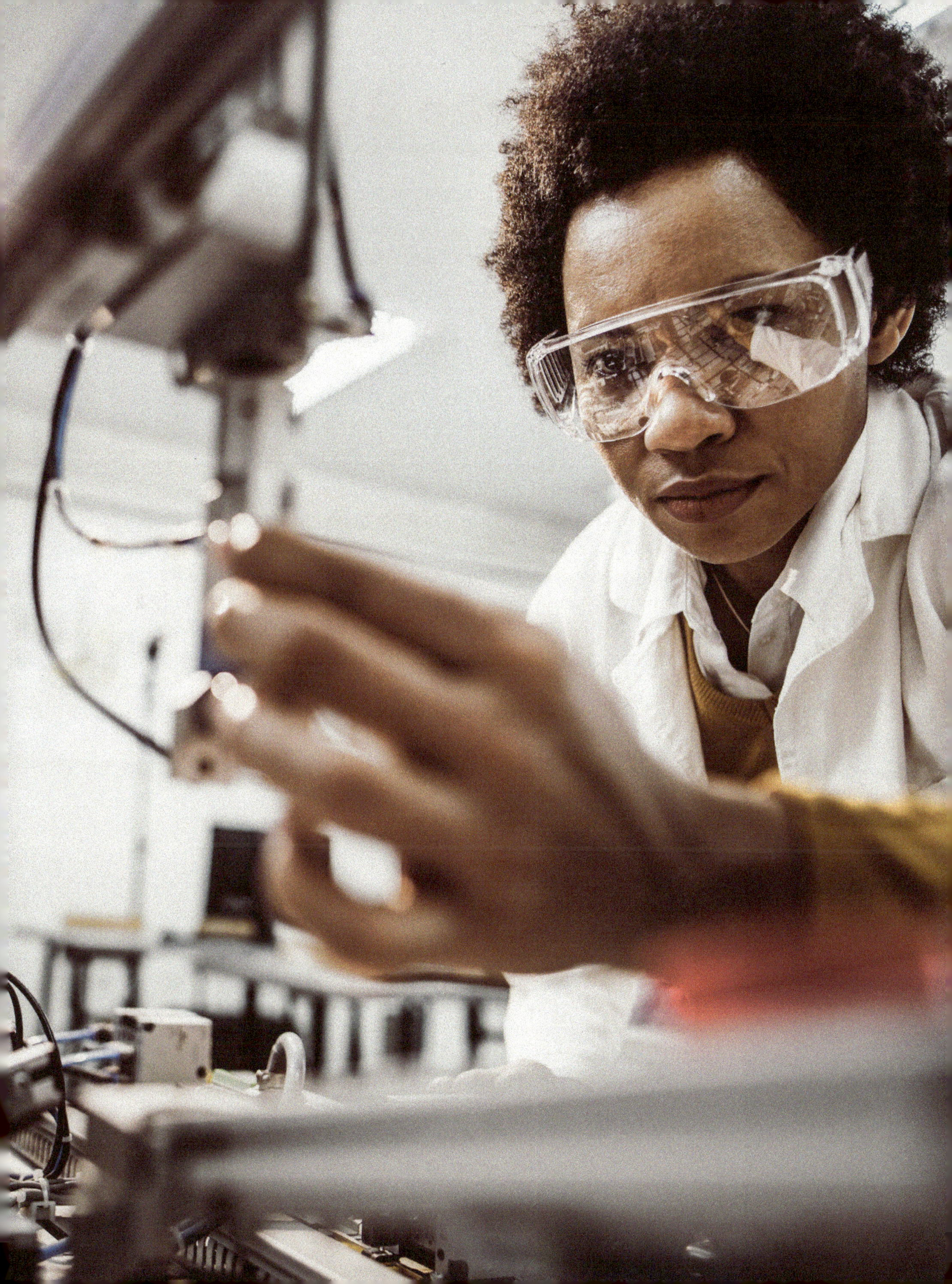

Rockin' Rube Goldberg

Time: 20 minutes (or more)

The original idea: Have you ever heard of a Rube Goldberg machine? Rube Goldberg was an inventor and cartoonist who was born 1883. He was known for drawing machines that solved simple tasks in the most complicated but hilarious ways. Simple machines made of pulleys, levers, and inclined planes were used to make his drawings interesting and whimsical. As complex and detailed as his drawings were, Rube Goldberg never actually built any of his designs. We could use Rube Goldberg–inspired drawings to create a machine that makes pancakes or brushes our teeth, but it's best to start with a simple concept, like flipping a light switch or closing a door.

Let's get started! Find something that can roll, like a toy car or a rubber ball, and pair it with something that can fall, maybe wooden blocks, dominoes, or LEGO pieces. Line up your blocks in a row that will fall, one by one, and test them out by pushing them over with your hand. If you have a reliable formation, start experimenting with rolling an object with enough force to knock the first block down. Experimenting with the steps, one at a time, will help you be more successful when your machine becomes more complicated.

CAUTION: Try to avoid building where people could trip on your materials. Use caution when building on stairs or near doors.

Materials

You can use almost any material that you have around your home. Here are some examples:

- Dominoes
- String or yarn
- Cardboard tubes or recycled cardboard pieces
- A fan
- Rubber balls
- Marbles
- Cups
- Rulers
- Tubes

The Steps

1. First, think about the simple task that you'd like to accomplish. If you've seen a Rube Goldberg machine in a movie or TV show, it can be your inspiration! Ask a grown-up if you can look up some examples or plan a brainstorm together about your machine. Ask a grown-up if you can look up some examples or brainstorm together about your machine.

2. Start experimenting with your Rube Goldberg machine, one step at a time. Let's start with three simple steps to get going. Find a small ball (a tennis ball works), a disposable cup, and some LEGOs, dominoes, or plank blocks that can make each other fall.

3. Put the ball inside of the cup and carefully line up your blocks so that the ball will knock them over when the cup is tipped.

4. Now gently tip over the cup and see if the ball rolls into your blocks. Did it work? You may have to adjust the distance or force you are using. Mark off areas of your floor with masking tape so that you can try this a few times.

5. When you can get it to work consistently, try to add another component! What would make the cup tip over with the same force as your hand?

6. Try to get at least three components of your machine working. Can you do it? Does the machine accomplish your original goal?

Observations

- Which part of your machine works most consistently? Which is the most unreliable?
- How can you use materials in new ways?
- Which is your favorite part of the machine? Which is the most frustrating?

Modernize It

What high-tech pieces can you use to make your machine more precise or powerful? If you have motors or gears from a robotics kit, you can try to incorporate them here. What else can you use? Ask a grown-up to look up some Rube Goldberg videos online for you to watch as inspiration for your machine.

The Hows & Whys

Sometimes, the greatest discoveries happen by accident. Albert Einstein once said, "Play is the highest form of research." Don't be afraid to get creative and try something new, even if you don't think it will work!

Link for reference

www.rubegoldberg.com/rube-the-artist/

Observations

_____
_____
_____
_____
_____
_____
_____
_____
_____
_____
_____
_____

> *Rube Goldberg always picked the simplest tasks and made them more complicated. You can try flipping a light switch, closing a door, putting dog food into a bowl, anything you can think of—it's really up to you.*

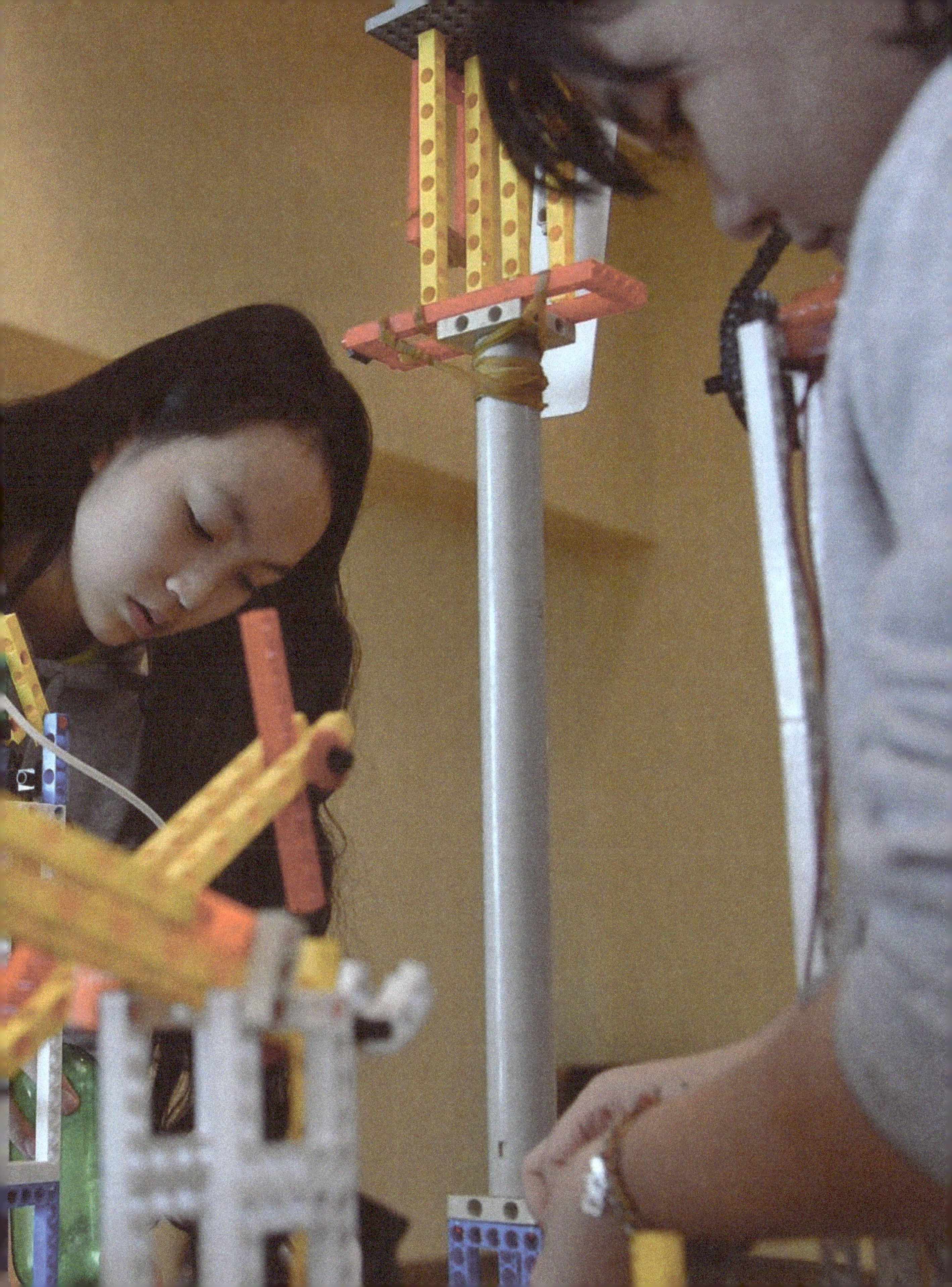

Decisions & Designs

Time: 20 minutes (or more)

The original idea: We're going to use the design thinking steps from part 3 (see page 90–91) to help you find a workable idea to solve a problem and brainstorm ideas for prototypes. Design thinking in a group is easiest when done with materials that can help the conversation flow and where everyone can contribute.

Materials

- Poster board
- Notebook
- Markers, pens, and pencils
- Library card
- Sticky notes

The Steps

1. **Empathize:** Take out your notebook and write down some issues that affect you or your community that you'd like to see change. For instance, you could see trash that litters your library parking lot or a neighborhood animal rescue shelter in need of beds and toys. Pick an issue that you would like to help resolve. You can interview people directly affected by the problem to understand their wants and needs. Their feedback will give you ideas to get you started.

2. **Define:** Once you complete your research, define the specific problem you want to solve. For instance, if there is litter in the library parking lot, are you hoping to clean up what is there now or prevent more in the future? Make very specific notes about the problem you want to solve.

3. **Ideate:** It's time to brainstorm creative solutions to your problem. You can write each idea on a sticky note and stick them on a wall. Sometimes, looking at all of the possible solutions can help you think up the perfect one.

The Hows & Whys

You've heard the expression two brains are better than one, right? When using design thinking in a group, it's important that you make sure everyone's contributions are heard and written in your notebook. This will help you find a common solution to the problem you're trying to solve.

Observations

Design thinking is an organized way to come up with good ideas by yourself or with a group of people.

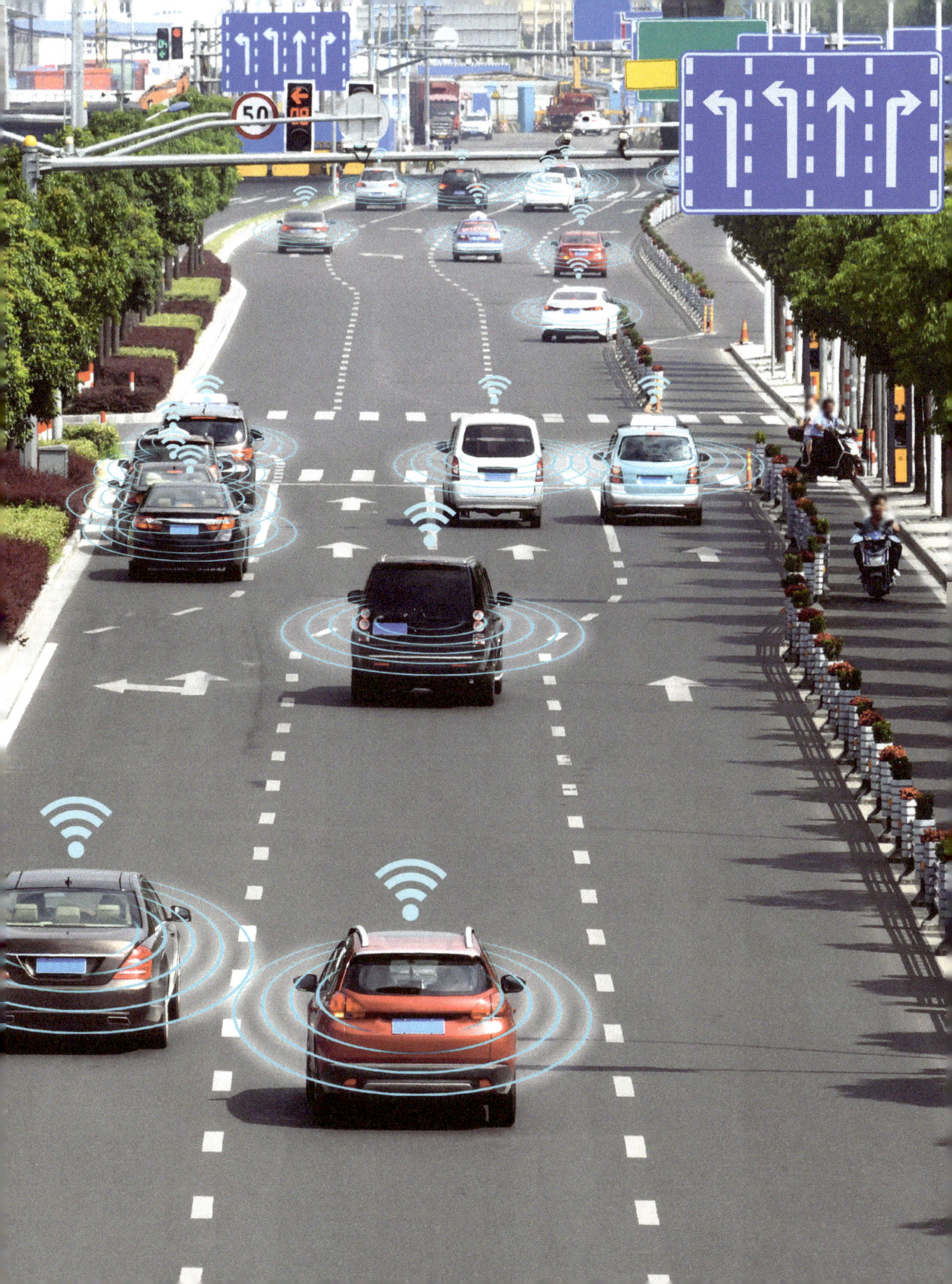
50

Decisions & Designs Part II: The Prototype

Time: 15 to 20 minutes

The original idea: Now, it's time to make a prototype. You can start by sketching your plans on a piece of paper and describing the materials you will use, making notes on each feature you'll build. Using your design thinking notes, you can create a prototype to solve your problem.

CAUTION: Ask for permission before taking any materials for use in your prototype.

Materials

- Anything that you can find can work for your project. Here are a few examples:
- Markers, pens, or pencils
- String or yarn
- Cardboard tubes or recycled carboard pieces
- Rubber balls
- Marbles
- Cups
- Rulers
- Tubes
- Wheels

The Steps

1. Using common objects in your home or at school, make a simple model of your problem-solving design. Begin by sketching in your notebook or on larger pieces of paper. Then, gather materials to bring the sketch to life. Using the example of the trash-riddled library parking lot, your prototype could be a divided trash bin for garbage and different types of recycling, or it could be a design for signs that you could post in the parking lot to encourage people to throw their garbage away in the proper bins. The goal here is not perfection. The idea is to experiment with different materials in creative ways. And there is no rule for how many prototypes you can design to solve your dilemma.

2. Test your idea by asking a few friends for their feedback. Don't be discouraged if they don't find it as useful as you'd hoped. In fact, that constructive criticism is valuable, as it helps you find any flaws in your design that you need to iron out. Use their feedback to tinker with your prototype and make it even better.

Modernize It

If you're able, you can start to design parts of your prototype on Tinkercad, and if you have access to a 3D printer at school or a local library, you can ask for help printing it out.

The Hows & Whys

Design thinking is a valuable process used by engineers in their work. You can apply it to both simple and complex projects as you experiment with prototypes and innovations.

Observations

Remember, design thinking in a group means letting the conversation flow and inviting everyone to contribute.

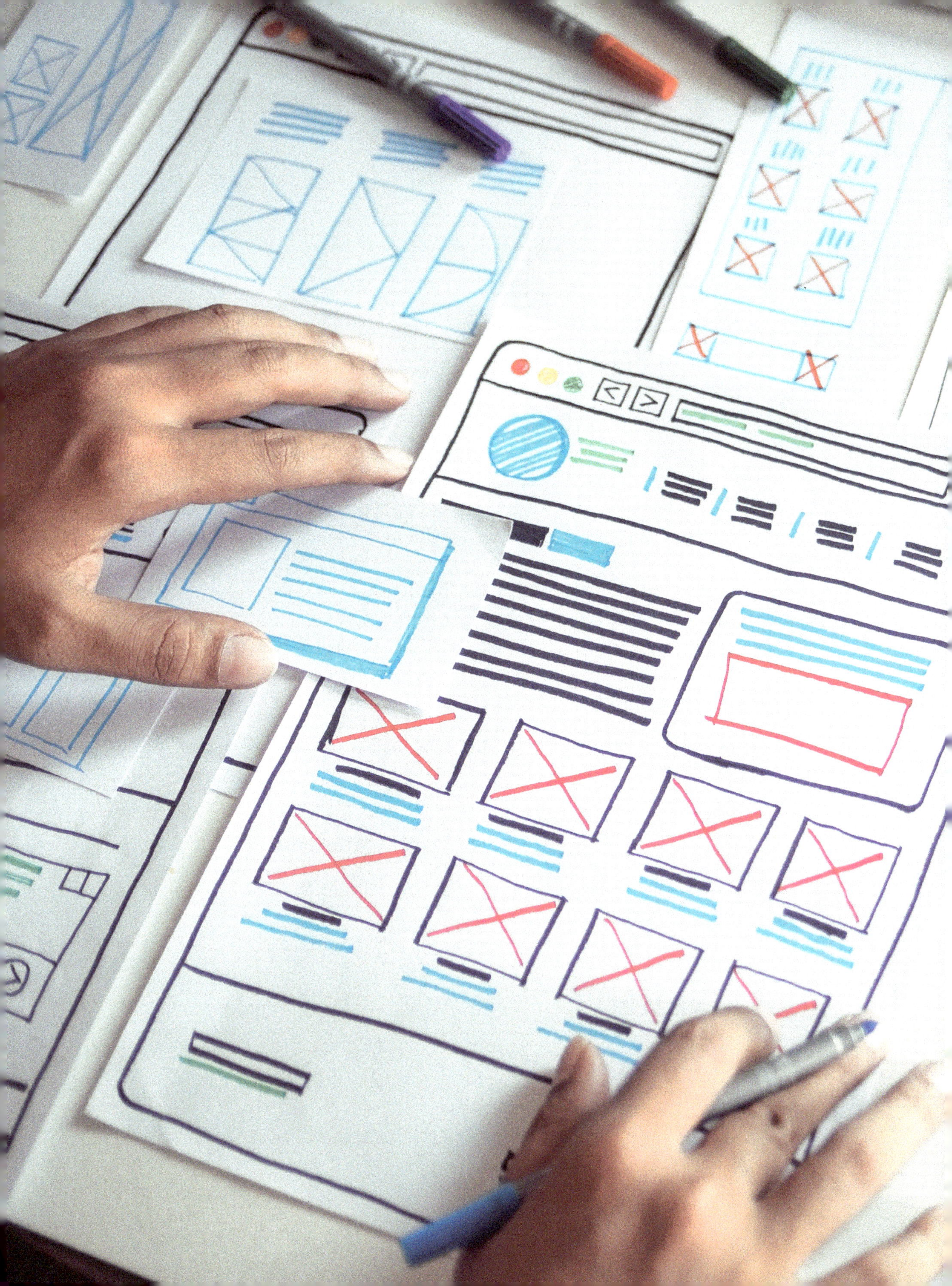

Changemakers Made Visible: A Research Project

Time: 20 minutes (or more)

The original idea: The work we do with computers and modern tech is enhanced by what we do offline. Engineers and inventors spend a great deal of time away from their screens reading and writing. Researching the past helps us prepare for the innovations of the future.

One worthy aspect of this is learning about the innovators who came before us. So many of the groundbreaking innovators in the history of technology were made invisible, meaning they were never recognized for their accomplishments. Many were discriminated against because of their race or gender and had to fight for their education and ideas. One notable figure was Katherine Johnson, a brilliant NASA mathematician who calculated space flight projections by hand. Katherine Johnson's hard work and contributions to space flight would have gone unrecognized if it weren't for the work of historians who amplified her legacy and made her contributions visible for the world to admire.

In this project, you will research a person who has greatly contributed to technological evolution that others may not know about.

Here are some names to get you started:

- Otis Boykin
- Marie Van Brittan Brown
- Marian R. Croak
- Annie Easley
- Lisa Gelobter
- Ayanna Howard
- Shirley Ann Jackson
- Lonnie G. Johnson
- Hedy Lamarr

Research Questions

- When was your changemaker born? Where did they live? What was their background?
- What is your changemaker known for? How did they make an impact on the world of technology?
- Did your changemaker experience hardships during their career? How did they work past them?

Modernize It

You can make a poster with facts about your changemaker. If you have access to a computer, use Scratch (scratch.mit.edu/) to animate your project. There are some great historical projects made by kids on Scratch that you can draw inspiration from. Educate your friends and family about your changemaker. This history is meaningful, and by sharing it, you can help make the invisible visible.

The Hows & Whys

A big part of making the world a better place is amplifying the voices of those who are trying to do just that. Highlighting a changemaker is a good way to practice equality in the technology field and a great way to promote tech for good.

Observations

Hedy Lamarr was a household name in the 1930s for starring in some of Hollywood's biggest hits, but few realize that the Austrian-American co-invented the "frequency hopping" technology that would make Wi-Fi, GPS, and bluetooth possible.

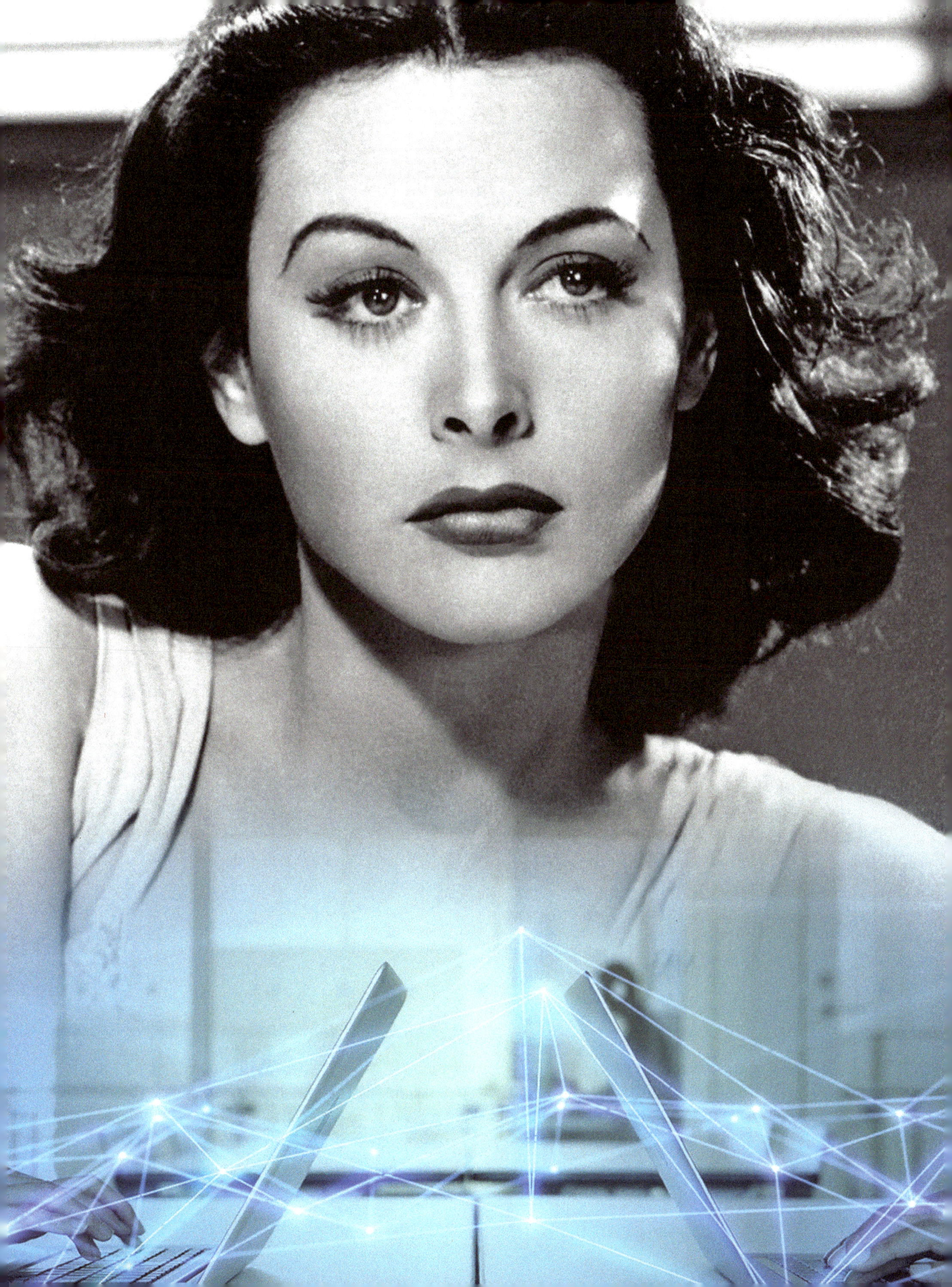

It's Not What You Want to Be, It's What You Want to DO

You may have been asked the following question once or twice in your lifetime: "What do you want to be when you grow up?" In fact, you may have been asked several times by now. It is a question adults tend to ask, but it doesn't mean that you have to wait to get started on your dreams.

One of the wonderful things about the internet is that it provides an unlimited amount of resources to learn from, no matter what your dream may be. You can use the resources listed in this book to get started. You can also talk with your teachers and grown-ups about topics you're interested in learning about. You are in charge of your own education and deserve every opportunity to learn and explore your interests.

Make a list of classes you'd like to take or hobbies you may want to try. If you know someone who is an engineer, ask them how they got started and what they were interested in as a kid. Technology can help you pursue almost anything that you're interested in. Maybe you like to create art. Explore design programs like Tinkercad and tools like 3D pens to make mixed-media art or photography projects. Maybe you're interested in acting or directing. You can use your camera and computer software to make your very own movie. The possibilities are endless, and everything you create will be filled with all the same magic and wonder that you are, so get started.

What will you code, invent, or create, to bring positive change to our world?

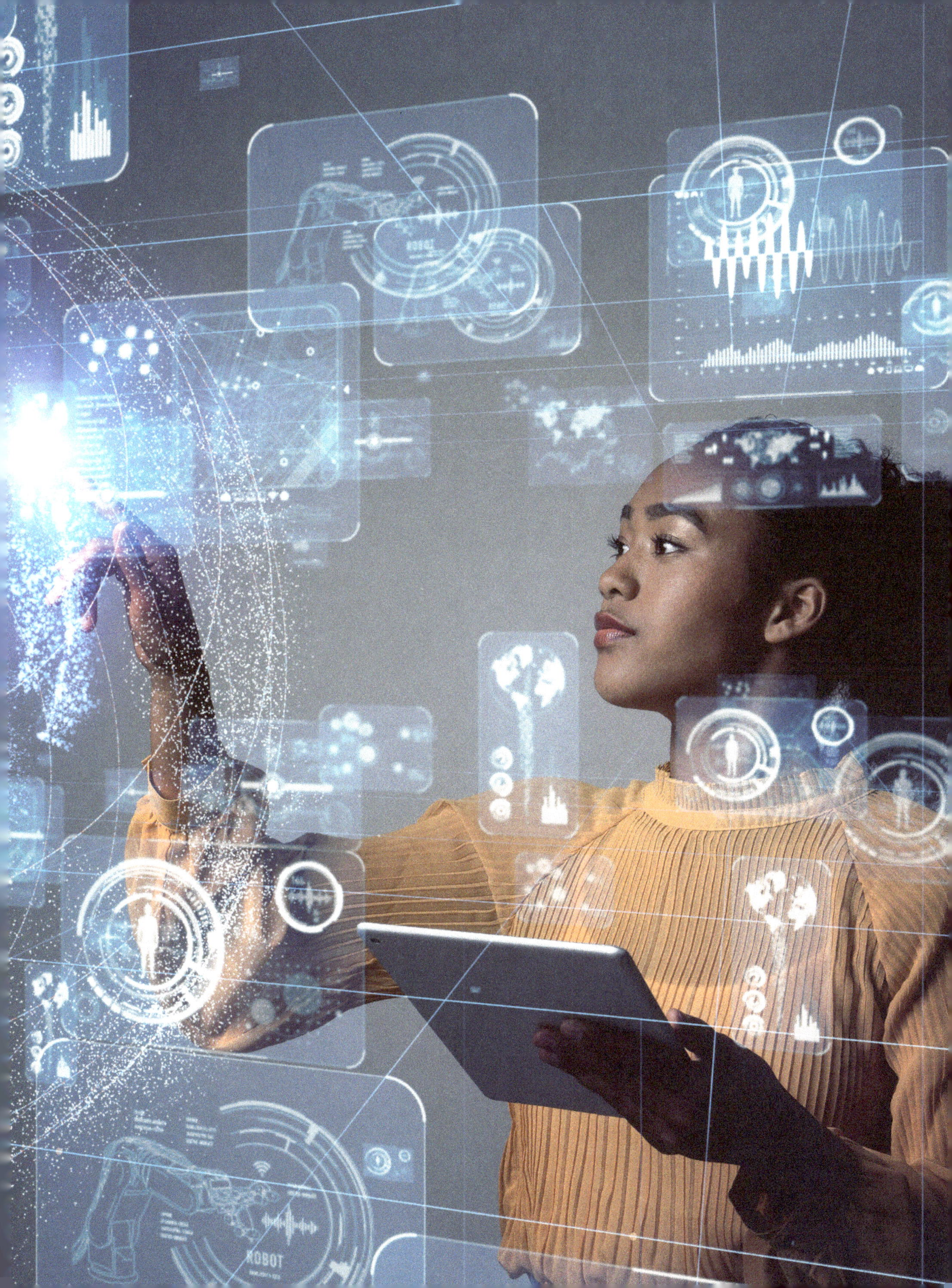
ROBOT

Glossary

artificial intelligence (AI) – a computer's ability to think or learn from the information it is given

augmented reality (AR) – tech that brings the virtual and real worlds together

automation – a process that is done automatically by a machine without human help

autonomous – operating independently without direct control from a human

axes – the first three dimensions: length, width, and height, referred to as X, Y, and Z

binary code – a coding system composed of 1s and 0s

biomimetics – the study how different animals move, swim, grab, and jump that roboticists use to gain inspiration for their own machines

brainstorm – to generate ideas individually or as a group

cloud – a place where digital information is stored, away from your device

computer – a person who computes mathematical equations or an electronic machine that processes data

computer programmer – someone who writes computer programs

constructive feedback – specific and helpful information

data – information

define – to explain

design thinking – problem-solving done by thinking deeply and specifically

digital assistants – devices that follow instructions and perform tasks using voice commands

drone – an autonomous aerial vehicle

empathize – to understand someone else's feelings

ethical – the right thing to do

filament – a material made from plastic used in 3D printing

G-Code – the path or program that tells a machine how to move

hardware – the physical parts of a computer or robot

humanoid – a robot built in a human form

ideate – coming up with creative solutions to solve your problem

inception – creation

innovate – to introduce something new to the world

innovation – a great new idea

intellectual property (IP) – creative works like photographs, drawings, films, and music

Internet of Things (IOT) – the ability to send and receive information between different kinds of devices using the internet

iteration – a newer or better version created after repeating a process many times

loom – a device to weave yarn to make clothes and other fabrics

loop – to perform a repeated action

machine learning – the usage of patterns and similarities to teach computers

origin – history

packets – pieces of data

packet switching – sending information from one computer to another online

pair – to link

path – a program

pictograph – ancient emojis; communication using symbols

program – the set of instructions that tells a computer what to do

prototype – a simple model of your idea that you can share

punch cards – flat, rectangular pieces of paper with small holes cut out in specific patterns

replica – a model

robot – a machine that uses sensors to evaluate its environment, make decisions, and act

roboticist – a robot designer

sensors – tools that robots use to gather information about the world around them

smart device – a device connected to the internet that can send and receive information

software – the program or directions that hardware follows

STEM – an acronym for science, technology, engineering, and mathematics

test – to try out

textiles – clothes or other woven fabrics

ultrasonic sensor – a sensor that uses ultrasonic sound waves to figure out its position relative to other objects

virtual reality (VR) – the use of computer technology to create a simulated environment

wake word – the word that will wake a virtual assistant

wearables – devices that you wear on your body

Resources

Here are a few resources to help you learn more about tech.

Websites

Scratch: a great place to start your coding journey
www.scratch.mit.edu

Code.org: learn lots of new coding languages
www.code.org

Khan Academy: a good resource for many topics you can learn on your own, including science and technology
www.khanacademy.org

Tinkercad: an easy-to-use site that will teach you how to make 3D models
www.tinkercad.com

Instructables: lots of STEM project tutorials made with a variety of fun materials
www.instructables.com

Girls Who Code: www.girlswhocode.com

First LEGO League: www.firstlegoleague.org

Robots

Sphero: programmable robots for kids in various shapes
www.sphero.com

Ozobot: tiny robots that can be programmed in many ways, including with your very own art
www.ozobot.com

Acknowledgments

First and foremost, I want to thank my parents for their unwavering love and support. I am here because of their prayers and their continuous and wholehearted belief in my every wish, hope, and dream. I will never find words to express how deep my gratitude runs for my parents, and I love them more than anything in this life. I especially want to thank my father, Philip, who spent 43 years in the publishing industry as a journalist and editor. I am so inspired by his career, and he is the best writer and poet that I've ever known. He has encouraged me through every step of this journey, and I am eternally grateful.

I owe so much to the faculty and staff of Carnegie Mellon University. I know that my educational experience has played a crucial role in my work. I want to thank two of my college professors, Dr. Edda Fields-Black and Dr. Joseph Trotter, for their support during my college years and the opportunity to be a research associate as they wrote their books.

I want to thank Reshma Saujani and the entire Girls Who Code community for their unwavering commitment to closing the gender gap in tech. Thank you to my own Girls Who Code club and co-facilitators; you girls are everything to me, and you inspire me to keep pushing for a better future even when it gets tough. And a big thank you to my editor, Morgan Shanahan, for absolutely everything that you have done to make this book come to life.

About the Author

Chloe Taylor is an author and entrepreneur based in Brooklyn, New York. She is the founder of Chloe Taylor Technology, a STEM education consulting company that partners with schools, businesses, and organizations looking to incorporate technology education for young learners. She is originally from Pittsburgh, Pennsylvania, and a graduate of Carnegie Mellon University, where she completed her undergraduate studies and an additional certification at the National Robotics Engineering Center (NREC).

Chloe has been a facilitator of the Girls Who Code program for four years and is a passionate advocate for gender and racial equity in the technology industry. She speaks to youth and adult groups about the importance of STEM education and
finding professional passion.

Find more about Chloe online at ChloeTaylorTech.com and on social media @ChloeTaylorTech.

CPSIA information can be obtained
at www.ICGtesting.com
Printed in the USA
JSHW040239030720
6431JS00005B/19

9 781646 112517